FRIENDS IN CHRIST

FRIENDS IN CHRIST

PATHS TO A
NEW UNDERSTANDING OF
CHURCH

Brother John of Taizé

ORBIS BOOKS
Maryknoll, New York 10545

Copyright © 2012 by Ateliers et Presses de Taizé, 71250 Taizé, France.
Original French version © 2011 Ateliers et Presses de Taizé, 71250 Taizé, France
English version by Brother John of Taizé.

Published in English by Orbis Books, Maryknoll, New York 10545-0302.
Manufactured in the United States of America.

Published in French by Ateliers et Presses de Taizé as *Une multitude d'amis: Réimaginer l'Église chrétienne à l'heure de la mondialisation.*

Library of Congress Cataloging-in-Publication Data

John, de Taize, Brother
  Friends in Christ: paths to a new understanding of church / Brother John of Taize.
    p. cm.
  Includes bibliographical references.
   ISBN 978-1-62698-000-6 (pbk.); eISBN 978-1-60833-235-9 (ebook)
   1. Friendship—Religious aspects—Christianity. I. Title.
BV4647.F7J624 2012
262'.7—dc23

                                                                2012012883

CONTENTS

For the sake of my brothers and my friends
I will say: Peace be yours!
For the sake of the house of the Lord our God
I will seek your good.

(Psalm 122:8-9)

Introduction

The inspiration for this book came from a personal experience. A few years ago, I was traveling alone in Italy. I went there, as I often do, to visit groups of young people we know, to continue a common search with them through times of prayer and sharing. Since I was in a different city almost every day, I often heard remarks like "It must be hard for you to travel like this. Don't you feel lonely, so far from your community?"

Such a thought had never even crossed my mind, and so I usually replied, "Feel lonely? Wherever I go I am welcomed by so many friends!"

Friends everywhere. . . . Upon reflection, I said to myself that the young and not-so-young people I was spending time with were not just my personal friends; our relationship was rooted in experiences shared in Taizé and in other meetings where participants come to deepen their faith and discover the meaning of being together because of Christ. Did not Jesus himself say, "I call you friends" (John 15:15)? If we are all friends of Jesus, I thought, then we are also friends of one another. This insight led me to reflect on the theme of friendship as a way of coming to understand better the message of Jesus Christ.

Friendship as such does not, it is true, play a major role in the Bible. In the New Testament, to describe the bonds between believers, it is largely eclipsed by other images taken, above all, from family life but also from the human body, the construction of a building, and so forth. The topic of friendship is nonetheless present, if somewhat hidden beneath the surface. It springs up again and again throughout the history of Christianity. In our day, in a civilization where almost all the institutions are undergoing a crisis of meaning, it may have more significance than many other kinds of human relations. The younger generations, in any case, still seem to be searching for friendship. Even if it is currently in danger of being distorted or perverted by a society based exclusively on profit, efficiency, and consumption, for the moment it remains—along with and perhaps even more than the family—one of the havens where our humanity is able to affirm itself in an ever more dehumanized world.

The friendship that many discover at Taizé and in similar situations has a special quality, however: it is not limited to a small group of individuals, all with the same background and convictions in common. In this too it corresponds to a feature of the contemporary world. Like it or not, we are all involved in a vast process generally referred to as globalization. If humankind is on the road to discovering its unity to an ever greater degree, is it not manifesting a dimension that is already implicit in the Christian faith? It may be, then, that the current evolutions of human society can help us to grasp more clearly certain aspects that belong, by right, to our own spiritual heritage, to exercise our imagination on a par with our faith. Such a possibility was indicated by the words attributed to Pope John XXIII on his deathbed: it is not the Gospel that has changed; we are the ones who are beginning to understand it better. If that is the case, then, by a sort of feedback or boomerang effect, it is to be hoped that the Good News of Jesus Christ, rediscovered in all its magnitude and beauty, can give a positive orientation to the present-day aspirations toward one human family.

This book, therefore, wishes to shed light on the Christian message using the concept, paradoxical in human terms, of universal friendship. It begins with the question, "What is distinctive about the Christian faith?" This leads to the discovery of the notion of communion and thus of the importance of believers gathered together as church. A subsequent section explores the idea of friendship and the transformations it has undergone as a result of Christianity. There follows a chapter devoted to the adventure of Taizé and its founder, taken as a concrete example, or better a parable, of what a vast fabric of friends for the sake of Christ and the Gospel could look like. Finally, based on all that has been discovered, the book attempts to draw some practical conclusions for the life of Christians in today's world.

This book came into being in a monastic community that each year welcomes tens of thousands of young people from the most diverse backgrounds, searching for meaning in their lives. This ecumenical and international context has determined its orientation to a very great extent. Though the Catholic and American origins of its author have naturally exercised an influence on the questions asked and the way answers are sought, it does not wish to advocate partisan solutions but to stimulate as wide a reflection as possible. The author is also responsible for the translations of passages from Scripture and any other texts, where not otherwise indicated.

At the beginning of this new century, we sometimes have the impression that our world has entered into a long period of transition whose outcome is still hard to fathom. The conviction expressed here is that the Christian church, to the extent that it becomes aware of its identity as a worldwide network of friendship, can play a highly beneficial role in a world searching, often blindly, for its identity and unity. To make this possible there is only one way open to us: a return to the sources.

Taizé, August 20, 2010

1

The Christian Faith[1]

Before examining the importance of friendship and its relation to the church, we need to address a much more fundamental question. What in fact is this Christian faith that we profess? How can we define its distinctive character? Does it lie in baptism, in the creed we sometimes recite, or in particular moral values? Does following certain practices, such as going to church on Sunday morning, make one a Christian? Does it mean having certain specific ideas about the world or human life? Let us begin by attempting to answer this crucial question in successive stages.

A RELIGION?

If this question were asked point-blank of people selected at random, the answer would certainly be "Christianity is a *religion*; indeed, it is one of the major religions of the world today."

This reply, however evident it may be in the minds of many, is basically a modern and Western view of things. For its definition of religion as referring to "a particular system of faith and worship," the *Oxford English Dictionary* gives no examples before

1300, and most of the quotations come from 1560 on. The word
existed earlier in the Latin-speaking world, to be sure, but meant
rather scrupulous attention, respect for the sacred, veneration of
the gods; in the Christian era, it referred first of all to the choice
of a particular way of life, that of a monk or nun.[2] Similarly, the
word in English was first simply applied to monastic orders. It
was only in modern times, thanks in part to the progress of the
social sciences in the West, that there arose a notion of the world
as divided into several different "religions"—Christianity, Hin-
duism, Buddhism, Judaism, animism and so on—each one giving different and parallel answers to the same human questions
and needs. And if, at first, the different religions were viewed as
inseparable from the civilizations that gave rise to them, today
we tend more and more to detach them from their lands of origin
and to make them the simple object of personal choice. No one
raises their eyebrows any longer when someone who comes from
a Jewish family in Florida declares himself a Buddhist without
ever having set foot in a Far Eastern country.

There is admittedly something in this notion of "religions"
that corresponds to the empirical situation of the contemporary
world. With respect to the question that concerns us, however, it
risks leading us astray, first of all, because it imports into the reality of the Christian faith a concept that is fundamentally foreign
to it. Neither Jesus of Nazareth nor his disciples had the faintest
idea that they were in the process of starting a "new religion."
First and foremost, whatever we may wish to say about his true
identity, Jesus was an itinerant Jewish preacher, fully integrated
into the life of his people. That is where we need to start in order to understand the historical movement that found its origin

in him. By putting into the same boat, so to speak, complex historical realities, such as Christianity, Buddhism, and Islam, we are in danger of misunderstanding the distinctive nature of each one and still more of their founders. Jesus, the Buddha, and Muhammad did not have the same self-understanding, nor did they make the same claims. If we are not careful, the enterprise of comparative religion can lead us to set in parallel realities that are essentially heterogeneous.

We will not find what is specific about Christian faith, then, in the fact that it is a religion. Even for more precise reasons, linked to the content of this faith, theologians have sometimes been very reticent about using this term. The German Lutheran pastor Dietrich Bonhoeffer, executed in 1945 by the Nazis for his activities in the resistance against Hitler, is emblematic in this sense. Bonhoeffer's reticence had at least two causes. First and foremost, religion by definition concerns only a part of human existence, whereas in his eyes, Christ Jesus had necessarily to be in relationship with the whole of life. All attempts to confine him to a restricted sphere, to limit him to particular times, places, or practices, could only distort the true meaning of his life and work. Writing from prison at the end of his life, Bonhoeffer said in words that have become famous, "Jesus does not call to a new religion, but to life" (letter of July 18, 1944). It should be emphasized that this was not a last-minute discovery of his, as can be seen from another statement that dates from 1928: "Christ is not the bringer of a new religion, but the bringer of God."[3]

Bonhoeffer was unwilling to identify faith in Jesus Christ with a religion because, in his eyes, the notion of religion was partial in another sense, too: it was not equally valuable at all times and places. In his last years, seeing around him people for whom religion did not seem to be a vital necessity, he sensed the advent of a society where religion would no longer play a decisive role in day-to-day life. Convinced that Christ had come for these individuals too, Bonhoeffer did not think it essential to try and reawaken in them a "need for religion" in order to lead them to Christ; he considered such an attempt demeaning. And he saw a parallel with the early Christians, who gradually realized that to accept and live the Good News of Jesus Christ it was not necessary first to become a Jew. During the final period of his life in prison, Bonhoeffer wrestled with the question of how to bear witness to Christ to a world that had "come of age," for which the consolations of religion held little interest. Although his reflections were unfortunately cut short by his death, and beyond the possible limits of his diagnosis of the contemporary world (in this new century "religion" seems more alive than ever, at least if we look at things from a global perspective), his conviction that the distinctive feature of the Christian faith was not connected to its "religious" character remains permanently relevant, and opens a way forward for our quest. "Jesus does not call to a new religion, but to life."[4]

A SPIRITUALITY?

In our day, another word that comes spontaneously to mind to describe Christian faith is *spirituality*. The term places the emphasis on a personal, inner journey, on convictions and practices that foster spiritual growth, on the gradual development and deepening of an inner life. And, in fact, when we read the New Testament, we see that Jesus began his ministry by calling people to follow him one by one, to pass through "the narrow gate" (Matthew 7:13f). Given that, for Christians, Jesus is not a mere figure of the past but, risen from the dead, continues to be present for and among his followers, we might well wish to situate the essential aspect of Christianity in a personal relationship between the individual believer and Christ Jesus. Each man and woman receives a unique call by which they set out in the steps of Christ—not outwardly, by walking along the roads of Galilee, but inwardly, by living out their life day after day in this relationship and this call.

It is perhaps interesting in this regard that one of the best-known works of Dietrich Bonhoeffer bears the German title *Nachfolge*, "discipleship" (in English *The Cost of Discipleship*). More generally, it is not the least of the merits of certain strands of Protestant Christianity to have emphasized strongly the personal relationship of the believer with his or her Lord and Savior, Jesus Christ, and to affirm that no institution or outward rite can replace this. Even if he is invisible to our bodily eyes, Christ is present for the believer just as he was for his disciples in Palestine two thousand years ago. In a certain sense he is even more present, because his presence is not limited to an outward contact: Saint Paul can go to the point of writing that "I live, yet no longer I: Christ is living in me" (Galatians 2:20). Certainly, all the Christian traditions are familiar with this truth. It is enough to recall that the best-known work of spirituality in the West from the fifteenth century onward was *The Imitation of Christ* or to consider the importance of contemplating the icon of the face of Christ in the Eastern churches. Admitting all this, it is nonetheless Protestantism that has brought out most unambiguously the importance of devotion to the person of Jesus and of a personal response to his call.

The Christian faith can be understood as a spirituality from another angle as well, by identifying it with the "life according to the Spirit" which Saint Paul describes, notably in chapter 8 of his Letter to the Romans. If, for him, faith in Jesus Christ begins as a gift, the free gift of God's love to human beings who could never have earned or acquired it,[5] it is equally true that this gift has to be accepted by a free human choice. The God revealed by Jesus Christ never forces the human heart, and true love solicits and awakens a free response. The gift of God communicated by Christ thus corresponds to the reception of this gift on the part of human beings and the attempt to put it into practice. And since this gift is, above all, that of a breath of life (translated in our Bibles by the word "Spirit"), the only way to receive it is to make it our own life, to begin "breathing."

In short, Christianity can be seen as a spirituality to the extent that it is a venture rooted in what the Bible calls the human heart. We are invited to welcome love into the depths of our being and respond to it, translating this love into concrete choices in our day-to-day existence.

There are some drawbacks, however, in employing the notion of spirituality to define faith in Jesus Christ. In today's world, this notion often has eclectic and individualistic connotations. People tend to borrow elements taken from the most diverse horizons, leaving aside anything that does not mirror their own taste. Such a made-to-order spirituality does not correspond to what is distinctive in Christian faith. As we have seen, faith is essentially a relationship with the person of Christ rather than an acceptance of disparate doctrines. The main thing is the trust placed in him, beyond what we can understand from the outset. As was already the case with Abraham, believers consent to setting out on the road without knowing where they are heading (see Hebrews 11:8), sustained solely by faith in the One who calls them and walks with them. To borrow a phrase dear to Brother Roger, the founder of Taizé, faith is a permanent invitation to "live beyond every hope."

In addition, the Christian faith is not an individualistic endeavor. Whoever hears Christ's call and answers it takes his or her place in the community of all those walking along the same road. The relations between the disciples are just as important as the one with the Master, because they express in tangible fashion, beyond words, the content of their faith in Jesus. In this respect it may be useful to make a distinction between the words "personal" and "individual." Faith is eminently personal, based, as it is, on a unique call and an intimate relationship of trust with Christ; in a word, it is rooted in the heart. But this faith is not solely an individual affair, because it immediately inserts the believer into a network of relationships by making him or her a full-fledged member of the family of God.

A LIFE IN COMMON?

"Jesus does not call to a new religion, but to life." If Christianity indisputably possesses elements that could be called religious, since it places its followers in relation to the Absolute, and if in some respects it resembles a personal spirituality, it would be closer to the mark to see it as a way of life, more specifically a *life in common.* What made an impression on the inhabitants of the Mediterranean basin two thousand years ago was seeing people from the most varied backgrounds, languages, and social classes call one another brother and sister, and live a shared life, "Jews and Greeks, slaves and free, men and women" all together (cf. Galatians 3:28). And again, "There is no longer Greek and Jew, circumcised and uncircumcised, barbarian, Scythian, slave, free" (Colossians 3:11). Although there were some philosophical reflections on the unity of the human race in the ancient world, for the first time the dream of one human family began to acquire tangible form. And it can be argued that it was this lived-out reality, more than any particular doctrine, that gave early Christianity its power of attraction.

Three times in his book on the first Christians, The Acts of the Apostles, Saint Luke gives us a summary of their life. The first of these is found at the end of chapter 2, following the first Christian Pentecost:

> *They devoted themselves to the apostles' teaching and to the fellowship, to the breaking of the bread and to prayers. Everyone was in awe; many wonders and signs were taking place through the apostles. All the believers were united and held everything in common. They would sell their property and possessions and share them insofar as anyone was in need. They used to gather every day in the Temple by common consent and break bread in their homes, sharing food in gaiety and simplicity of heart, praising God and having the esteem of all the people. And day by day the Lord kept adding to their number those who were finding salvation. (Acts 2:42-47; cf. Acts 4:32-35, 5:12-16)*

What we see here essentially is a community living in the midst of the Jewish people (and soon called to go beyond the borders of that nation) and practicing two complementary forms of sharing: first with God, entailing an intense life of prayer that included traditional prayers and new practices, notably "the breaking of the bread," which refers in all likelihood to the Eucharist; and then among themselves, a sharing not just spiritual but material as well, to each according to their needs.

A somewhat idyllic impression emerges from this portrait. A closer reading of all the relevant texts concerning the early Christians shows that the reality was not always so perfect, in spite of the strong impetus given by the death and resurrection of Christ. Saint Luke does not describe the first Christian community in this way, however, because of a romantic or nostalgic bent, but rather to answer our question concerning what is distinctive about faith in Jesus Christ. It was not found so much in new ideas about God as in a shared existence. And according to Luke, it was this life in common that attracted people and explained the success of the new movement.

Another indication that, for Luke, we have here the essential dimension of the faith is given by the placing of this text at the end of chapter 2. We mentioned that Jesus was fully rooted in the people of Israel. This nation considered that it had received a particular vocation among all the nations on earth. The God who formed this people from a ragtag collection of immigrant workers in Egypt was not a mere tribal or local deity, but the Creator of the universe and the Lord of history. As a consequence, the historic role of the Jewish people was to witness by their existence to this God unlike any other so that, one day, all the nations of the earth would recognize him and thus live together in peace and harmony (see, e.g., Isaiah 2:2-4).

This vocation proper to Israel was hindered from the start by the vagaries of history. Many of the faithful, therefore, believed that a new beginning was necessary to realize it fully. This would involve a brand-new manifestation of God by which he would finally accomplish his original intention. The first disciples of Christ, after the apparent failure of his violent death, saw this new beginning in the Good News of the resurrection: the cause of Jesus was not over but in fact had just begun. It involved a new outpouring of the breath of divine life, the Spirit, to enable Israel to be what it had always been in God's mind from the very beginning: the nucleus of a renewed and reconciled humanity. So if Saint Luke begins his second book with Jesus, risen from the dead, sending the Holy Spirit upon his disciples to give new impetus to his mission after the interruption of his death, it is not surprising that he ends his narrative with the description of a community where this mission assumes a tangible shape.

In fact, the structure of the Acts of the Apostles is made up of two complementary movements. On the one hand, the followers of Christ are sent out on the highways and byways of the world to communicate the Good News to the four corners of the earth and create a network between those who respond to the call, and, on the other, they come together around the Lord's table, expressing by their unity the meaning and purpose of their mission. "How good and pleasant it is for brothers and sisters to live together in community!" (Psalm 133:1).

It is enlightening to superimpose these two movements characteristic of the early Christians upon the current situation of our churches. The outward movement of expansion has borne fruit in abundance. A powerful impulse toward this came from the fact that in the fourth century of our era, the Christian church went from being a disdained and even persecuted sect to having an officially recognized status in the Roman Empire. Parallel to this, Christian missionaries have brought the message everywhere, often at the cost of their lives. In short, Christianity has become a worldwide phenomenon.

If the major Christian denominations, beginning with the Catholic church, have thus grown to planetary dimensions, it has to be admitted that the aspect of coming together in unity has not known the same success. First of all, over the centuries the church of Jesus Christ has split up into segments indifferent or even hostile to one another and, in addition, the numerical and geographical progress of Christianity has apparently gone hand in hand with a diminishing of the intensity of its life. In dissolving into the mass, the salt of the Gospel has sometimes lost some of its saltiness or, to change the metaphor, the yeast seems to have vanished into the dough, at least for the time being. To find examples of communities known for an intense life of prayer and mutual support, one has to turn to the smaller evangelical or Pentecostal denominations or else to groups within the larger historical churches, for example, so-called monastic or religious communities, or what are known as the new ecclesial movements. And even then, these groups do not always bring together people from very different backgrounds. It is obviously very difficult, humanly speaking, to unite in practice universality and intimacy. In the portrait of the early Christians given in the New Testament, however, we do find just this, and from the very outset.

One sees groups that, on account of their faith in the crucified and risen Christ, share their existence fully with one another while remaining open to people from a great diversity of backgrounds. These groups retained a strong life of solidarity without becoming sectarian in the least, for they kept alive the conviction that they did not exist for themselves alone but had received a calling that concerned the whole human race, that of being a ferment of reconciliation and peace. In short, these communities held in harmony an intense common life and a universal outlook.

The standard word for this sharing of life is the Greek term *koinōnia*, translated into English as "fellowship" or "communion." Of all the New Testament writings, the prologue of the first letter of Saint John gives us the best key to its significance. Writing to people who entered the Christian community later than those of the first generation, the author speaks of Christ Jesus not as one individual among others but as "Life," "the Word of Life" or "eternal Life." In him, in other words, God's very own life has entered into human history in utterly tangible fashion. And he continues,

> *We proclaim in turn to you what we have seen and heard, so that you may have fellowship* (koinōnia) *with us. And our fellowship* (koinōnia) *is with the Father and with his Son Jesus Christ. We are writing these things to you so that our joy may be complete.* (1 John 1:3-4)

This word of life that has been communicated creates a *koinōnia*—a sharing of life, a solidarity—among those who receive it. And this shared existence is not a merely human reality, insofar as it is not based on the feelings or on the goodwill of the women and men involved. No, it is a participation in God's own life, in the communion that unites Christ with the one he calls *Abba*, Father, in the unity of one Spirit. And finally, Saint John says that this life shared among believers and with God is a source of true and perfect joy. If this is the case, is it not because it satisfies the deepest desire of human hearts, to be loved and to love with no restrictions in time and space?

THE OFFER IN PROGRESS OF A UNIVERSAL COMMUNION IN GOD

We are finally at the point where we can reply adequately to our question concerning what is distinctive about the Christian faith, having come closer to this answer by a series of more and more exact approximations. First of all, even if this faith has a "religious" dimension, since it concerns our relationship with that Absolute commonly called God, the notion of religion does not seem to be very helpful in order to grasp its unique character. Should it then be called a *spirituality?* Yes, in the sense that it offers a personal and lived-out way of plumbing the meaning of life more deeply. This way, however, is not left to the discretion of each individual; it is not made up of elements that we can take or leave according to our own whims. Far from being an aimless wandering amidst the flotsam and jetsam of the spiritual traditions of humankind, it is a pilgrimage in the steps of Christ, and it sets the pilgrim necessarily in a relationship to all those who are walking along the same road.

Is Christian faith a *life in common*, then? This definition has the great advantage of corresponding to the life of the early Christians as we discover it in the pages of the New Testament. Still, we must immediately add that this shared life is far from being a simple human sociability; it is rooted in God. It is a sharing in the divine life, a life that is love and thus life for others. As a result, already at its birth and even if its concrete manifestation is very limited, this common life is by nature inclusive, universal; it radiates outward to encompass potentially every human being. In this sense, the boundaries of the Christian community are not defined once and for all; in the final analysis they cannot be distinguished from the entire human family or even from the whole of creation.

In its essence, then, faith in Jesus Christ can be defined as *the offer in progress of a universal communion or fellowship in God*. Let us examine this definition more closely.

First of all, Christian faith, far from being a human undertaking, is essentially an *offer* or invitation coming from the side of God. This reversal of perspectives is, in fact, the "Copernican revolution" that characterizes all of biblical revelation. This was already true for Israel of old: that nation drew its identity not from geographical or genealogical criteria, but from the free choice of a mysterious and transcendent God. With the coming of Christ Jesus, this quality is even more salient. For his disciples—and here we have a situation virtually unique among the founders of religions or schools of spirituality—Jesus was not someone seized without warning by the divine or who attained enlightenment after a long process of searching; he was not in the first place a prophet, a teacher of wisdom, a philosopher or a seer. In him, however unthinkable this may seem, the very source of life comes to encounter us.

If the Christian faith is an offer coming from the side of the Absolute, the role of human beings is essentially to welcome the invitation and to reply to it. It is not up to them to define its contours. And if God calls, through Christ, to a sharing of life, to a communion, then this invitation is addressed to the most personal dimension of human beings; it seeks to awaken freedom in them. For all these reasons, such an offer is at the opposite extreme of every form of constraint. Any attempt to impose it by coercion, whether overt or subtle, is absolutely foreign to its nature. Alas, we all know that this truth has not always been grasped in the course of the centuries, either by Christian authorities or by the rank and file, to the great detriment of the true progress of the Gospel.

Secondly, the Christian message is an offer *in progress*, in other words an invitation that is real and not theoretical. It is not primarily a question of ideas, of a correct understanding of intellectual truths. In more technical terms, faith is not a gnosis. Just as Jesus communicated the essence of his message by his life given for us to the point of dying on a cross, disciples turn their own lives into the message they want to get across. As Saint Paul puts it, Christ gave his life for us "so that the living live no longer for themselves but for the one who died and rose for them" (2 Corinthians 5:15). And this existence "for Christ" translates into an existence "for others." We are thus led back again by a different road to the primacy of shared life. Christianity is perhaps unique in that, if it is not to be emptied of its substance, there can be no dichotomy between doctrine and practice. On the contrary, the doctrine is identical to the practice, for in both cases it is a matter of communion with God and among human beings. If Christians do not practice love for others, if the churches live in mutual indifference or competition, their preaching will inevitably remain a dead letter.

THE BODY OF CHRIST

We can recapitulate all we have discovered about the specificity of the Christian faith by drawing out the implications of some key notions of Saint Paul.

Let us begin with a question: what is the link between Christianity as a spirituality, as the imitation of Jesus, and as a life in common called to become more and more universal? Are these simply two different approaches, or is there a deeper logic that unites them?

A first element that helps us to discover this logic at work is the Semitic concept of the eponymous ancestor. For the world of the Bible, the founder of a people or a collectivity represents, in some sense, the entire group. Israel, for example, is a name used both for the patriarch Jacob and for the nation that sprang from his loins. The Israelites are "the sons (or children) of Israel" and the son is in his father's image (cf. Genesis 5:3). Similarly, for Saint Paul, Adam is not merely the first individual to have been created but at the same time the "founding father" of humankind. In a mysterious but real sense, Adam is each of us, and each of us is Adam. If "all have sinned" in him, this participation in his sin becomes concrete in the real choices that each of us makes in our own existence (see Romans 5).

This way of thinking gives the apostle a marvelous possibility to explain the relationship between Christ Jesus and us. There is

one small difference, however: unlike Adam or Israel, the followers of Christ are not *his* children but, through him, children of
God; we are sons (and daughters) in the Son. Through baptism,
which expresses Christ's call and our "yes" in response, we die
to our previous life marked by separation and enter the family of
God. In this way, Jesus is "the eldest of a multitude of brothers
and sisters" (Romans 8:29); he is in us and we are in him. "I live,
yet no longer I: Christ is living in me" (Galatians 2:20).

A second element concerns the notion of the body. Paul uses
it first as a metaphor, quite common at the time, of the Christian community. The relationship between the body and its various parts enables him to articulate the relationship between unity
and diversity in the community: animated by the same breath of
life, believers nonetheless still maintain a variety of gifts and approaches. This image emphasizes as well the close unity between
the faithful: "we are all parts of one another" (Romans 12:5).

In the apostle's mind, however, this explanation goes much
further than a simple metaphor. He writes to the Corinthians, "Just
as the body is one and has many parts, (...) so too is *Christ*" (1 Corinthians 12:12). Notice that he does not write "so too is our community" or "the church." And a bit further on he says explicitly, "*You*
are the body of Christ; each of you is a part of it" (1 Corinthians
12:27). In those days, the body was not conceived of as a lump of
flesh, as is often the case in our materialistic age, but as someone's
presence in the world, more precisely a presence to other people.
Calling the Christian community the Body of Christ thus means affirming that Christ remains present in the world through the shared
life of his followers. All together they re-present him, literally making him present in the world of space and time.

One more step, and we enter into the vast perspective of the letters to the Colossians and Ephesians. Both begin with the great design of God, which is "to recapitulate" (Ephesians 1:10) or "to reconcile" (Colossians 1:20) all creatures to himself, and consequently to one another, through Christ. The sign and the means of this double reconciliation is the communion of believers, the church, a reality in constant evolution, drawing its energy from its relationship to its Head, Christ Jesus:

Living according to the truth in love, we will grow up in all ways into Christ, the Head, through whom the whole body fits and holds together with the help of each joint, according to the working of each part, enabling the body to keep growing by building itself up in love. (Ephesians 4:15-16; cf. Colossians 2:19)

A body nailed to a cross in Palestine two thousand years ago, giving birth, on the other side of death, to a body that grows in the course of centuries by bringing together, in different ways, a countless number of women and men, and on the horizon, a vision of the whole of humankind as one family living in peace: this image expresses perhaps better than any other the distinctive identity of the Christian faith. To use an expression of Saint Augustine, one of the greatest Christian thinkers of the West, Christianity, in the final analysis, is nothing other than the *totus Christus*, the "whole Christ," Head and body, a reality that has also been called the "Christ of communion."

It is thus not by chance that the central activity of the Christian faith has always been the celebration of the Eucharist. The crucified Christ remains alive and present through the words he spoke over the bread and wine before his death: "This is my Body … This is my Blood." Gathered together around the same table, his followers are nourished by that body given for them on the cross and given to them in the sacrament, in order to be that body for others in the world. Nor it is a misuse of language to call this sacrament Holy Communion. In the Eucharist, the heart of the faith is expressed with unparalleled clarity. It is revealed there as a sharing of life with God, through Christ's self-giving, which unites us more closely among ourselves and sends us out to encounter every human being.

We can conclude our reflections with two quotes, the first from Dietrich Bonhoeffer and the second from Brother Roger. They sum up our discoveries well:

> *The Church is not about religion, but rather about the figure of Christ and its taking shape in a multitude of persons.*[6]

> *Are we sufficiently aware that, two thousand years ago, Christ came to earth not to start a new religion but to offer every human being a communion in God?*[7]

2

The Church

Let us recapitulate our findings. In the previous chapter, we began with a sociological and external view of Christianity as one religion or spirituality among others. Leaving this behind as insufficient, we finally came to understand it as *the offer in progress of a universal communion or fellowship in God*. By entering fully into the human condition through Jesus the Christ, his incarnate image, God invites all human beings to share in his own life. Those who accept this invitation are penetrated and transformed by the divine breath, the Holy Spirit. And this sharing and transformation, by its very nature, simultaneously transforms the relationship among human beings. They discover themselves to be participants in the same ongoing life, members of one human family or, as Saint Paul puts it even more incisively, parts of the same body (see Romans 12:5; 1 Corinthians 12:12f; Ephesians 5:30).

It should therefore be clear why no human categories already at hand are adequate for an understanding of the Christian faith. In order to comprehend it correctly, we must receive it on its own terms. But this immediately gives rise to another question: how did such a reality *sui generis*, one of a kind, arise in the midst of the human condition? If Christianity is an "offer in progress," that implies that by its nature it has a historical dimension; it evolves over time. Similarly, we may well suspect that it did not arrive one day on earth ready-made, like a meteorite falling from the sky, but rather that it came into being as the result of an ongoing development. This chapter, then, will look at the Christian faith not from a synchronic but from a diachronic perspective. In other words, it will attempt to sketch out the process by which human realities were taken up and gradually transformed in order to give birth to something utterly new in the history of our race, that unique communion called the church.

A People of Priests

Already in its foundational document, the Christian faith bears witness to its particular origins. The Christian Bible does not begin with the story of its founder, Jesus of Nazareth, but rather with the history of a people called Israel. In human terms, Israel appears to be one of the many small nations populating the Middle East two or three millennia ago, whose fate depended, above all, on the interplay between the great empires that rose and fell with almost predictable regularity. In its own self-understanding, however, this tiny people did not view itself as one among many, but as the bearer of a unique identity and mission. The Hebrew Scriptures, the "Old Testament" of Christians, tell a fascinating story about the God of the universe taking a group of slaves in Egypt and creating a people unlike any other (cf. Numbers 23:9). To describe this process, the biblical authors speak of God's *cov-*

enant, or pact, with those he liberated. "You have seen what I have done with the Egyptians and how I have carried you on eagle's wings and brought you to me. And now if you listen attentively to my voice and keep my covenant, you will belong to me out of all the peoples, for the whole world is mine. You will be for me a kingdom of priests and a holy nation" (Exodus 19:4-6). Israel thus saw itself as a nation existing not because of ethnic or geographical factors, but because of the particular relationship it had with the Source of life. In this special case, being a people and being God's people are one and the same reality.

The indissoluble unity between a relationship with the Source of life and a relationship with one's fellows, which lies at the very heart of the Christian message, is thus rooted in the oldest strata of the Bible. But the unity between these two dimensions goes deeper still. In order to express their God-given identity as a tangible sign of the divine presence at the heart of the world, the Israelites are enjoined to listen to God's call and put his commandments into practice. And the most important divine commandments do not deal with matters of religious practice and custom. Instead, they define precisely what it means for Israel to be a people. They aim essentially at establishing right relationships among human beings. The Ten Words (Exodus 20:1-17; Deuteronomy 5:1-22), the nucleus of the Law of Moses, describe a society that views itself as a large family, the family of God. In this context, the particular commandments are not understood as moralistic injunctions addressed to individuals; they are rather the conditions necessary to define a space of justice and freedom, where the fulfillment of each person entails the fulfillment of all.

We are witnessing here, in the history of a tiny nation, an

unprecedented step forward in the spiritual evolution of human-kind, and it is unfortunate that millennia of overfamiliarity cause us to take it for granted. The step can perhaps best be defined as the discovery of a new logic or structure of relationship: the shift from a dyadic to a triadic logic, with the metaphor of the couple giving way to that of the family.[8] In the final analysis one does not honor the deity directly, so to speak, by offerings, vows, and the whole panoply of religious practice. I honor God, above all, by living in right relationship with my fellows. Conversely, my relationship with my fellows is mediated by the fact that we all are members of the same collectivity defined by its relationship to God. On the road to God, of necessity I encounter other human beings, and in my dealings with other humans, God is infallibly present.

It was not only in Israel, to be sure, that a link between religion and ethics was forged; all the great traditions of humankind achieved it, each in its own way. And even the people of the Bible did not accomplish it overnight but through a centuries-long process involving many setbacks and oversights. The great prophets of the nation were constantly waging war against an outlook whereby worship, rather than being the expression of a whole way of life in accordance with God's will, was seen as an end in itself, ultimately as a self-justifying technique to ensure the good graces of the deity. In contrast to this theology, they proclaimed their conviction that only by living in solidarity with their fellows and learning to "cease to do evil and strive to do good, seek justice, defend the oppressed, stand up for the orphan and take the side of the widow" (Isaiah 1:16f) could believers fulfill their calling, that of communicating God's identity to the entire world, in other words of allowing God's name to be revealed as holy (cf. Ezekiel 36:23).

FULFILLING THE TORAH

As heir to this long tradition, Jesus had no intention of rejecting or neglecting it. "I have not come to set aside [the Torah], but to fulfill it" (Matthew 5:17). In so doing, he went beneath the surface of the biblical books in all their diversity and put his finger on the essential. Responding to a theologian's question concerning what God desires most ("the greatest commandment of all"), Jesus replied by speaking of love of God and love of neighbor (Mark 12:28-31). What is noteworthy here is that a question asking for a single answer receives a double response, and by that very fact the two are shown to be one. In other words, for Jesus love of God and love of neighbor are not two separate realities but sides of one and the same coin. One can never be set in opposition to, or given preference over, the other. The "god" I would encounter by turning away from my fellow human beings is not the living God. Alternatively, true concern for humankind inevitably leads to asking the question of our common belonging, of seeking the common wellspring that makes my neighbor truly an alter ego, another self.

Of all the New Testament books, it is perhaps the first letter of Saint John that expresses this triadic logic most succinctly. "Love consists in this, not that we loved God, but that he loved us and sent his Son for the forgiveness of our sins. Beloved, if God so loved us, we too ought to love—not God [dyadic logic], but—one another" (1 John 4:10-11). And he goes on to explain,

"If someone says they love God but hates their brother or sister, they are a liar. For anyone who does not love their brother or sister whom they see cannot love the God they do not see. (...) If we love one another, God remains in us and his love has come to perfection in us" (1 John 4:20, 12). The only infallible proof that we are in communion with the mystery of God is the active love we show to those around us. My brother or sister is thus the visible and efficacious sign—the sacrament—of God's invisible presence.[9]

This biblical outlook, finding its culmination in the Gospel of Jesus Christ, opens the door to a critique of "religion" parallel to that of Bonhoeffer or Barth (see pp. 15-16). It also gives rise to a difficult question: in a world where my relationship to the origin is essentially determined by the way I treat my fellow human beings, what place is left for "religion" conceived of as those practices that express a relationship to the divinity not mediated through others? Is it not enough to act justly in the world in order to fulfill the divine commandments? Has not theology, for all practical purposes, been swallowed up in anthropology?

An answer to these questions requires a return to the starting-point. "We love, because he loved us first" (1 John 4:19). If it is true that love only becomes tangible in interhuman relationships, it is equally true that this thing we call love has to be discovered, received, and incorporated into our existence. Despite what some may think, it is not a self-evident form of human behavior. What we spontaneously call love is at best a pale reflection of a reality that transcends all human understanding. "This is how we know what love is: Jesus laid down his life for us. And so we ought to lay down our lives—not for him [dyadic logic], but—for our brothers and sisters" (1 John 3:16). Our human generosity needs to be constantly transfigured and supported by "the Love which moves the sun and the other stars."[10]

Thus, in his Sermon on the Mount, that programmatic discourse that Matthew places at the beginning of his Gospel, Jesus tells his disciples that their right way of acting must be superior to that of the religious elites of the day (see Matthew 5:20). And this means not practicing the quintessential acts of religion—almsgiving, prayer, and fasting—like actors (*hypocritai*) putting on a show, solely in conformity to an exterior model and for the sake of human approbation (see Matthew 6:1-18). Instead, the disciples are called to discover "[their] Father, who is in the hidden place" (Matthew 6:6, 18). Jesus insists strongly on what today we would call a personal relationship with God. He reveals the Source of life not as some distant sovereign but as One who is a loving Abba (Father) and who can be found by turning inward. This is the One with whom we can and should engage in an intimate dialogue of prayer, who knows what we need and wants to give it to us (Matthew 6:6-8, 7:7-11).

In thus placing the accent on the discovery of an inward dimension, of that place that the Bible calls the heart, Jesus does not, for all that, reduce faith to a matter of attitudes and intentions. If the trap for his contemporaries was to limit their religion to outward conformity, the equally strong danger today is to turn that on its head and place the accent exclusively on inward states. "It doesn't matter what I do, or what church I go to, as long as my heart is in the right place." Jesus, for his part, insists on the unbreakable unity between the personal, inner relationship with God and outward behavior. To describe this, he employs the simple but profound image of a tree and its fruits (Matthew 7:16-20). In Jesus' eyes, this relationship with the Source is what enables one to "do the Father's will" (Matthew 7:21) in daily life. In the context of the Sermon on the Mount, Jesus' invitation to "ask and you will receive [from God]" (Matthew 7:7) refers specifically to the ability to "be perfect" (Matthew 5:48), in other words to fulfill the Torah by a love that extends even to those who respond not with love but with hatred.[11] Religion is thus not eliminated, but rather becomes the expression of a personal communion with God in Christ; it corresponds to the acts by which believers incorporate into their existence that divine life that is identical with love, God's own breath. Penetrated and transformed by that breath, they can then be wellsprings of love in their turn for all those entrusted to them.

WHO IS MY NEIGHBOR?

At the same time as he refocuses God's law by recapitulating it in the triadic logic of divine love, Jesus proclaims a no less radical extension of the recipients of that love. In the tradition handed down to him, the second great commandment "Love your neighbor as yourself" retained a certain ambiguity, for it included the implied question, which remained unanswered: "Who is my neighbor?" (Luke 10:29). In the original context of the Torah, the concept "neighbor" was identified with "the sons of your people," in other words one's fellow Israelite (Leviticus 19:18). It could also refer more specifically to one's kin ("your brother," Leviticus 19:17) or be widened to include the resident alien (*gēr*, Leviticus 19:34). In the later Jewish tradition, both restricted and expanded definitions of "neighbor" are found. In any case, the debate itself implicitly divides up human beings into two groups, as is clearly brought out in Jesus' explication of the commandment in the Sermon on the Mount: "You have heard that it was said: You will love your neighbor and hate your enemy" (Matthew 5:43). The commentaries unfailingly point out that the command to hate one's enemy (who in all probability, incidentally, was not a personal enemy but the adversary of those faithful to God and therefore the enemy of God; cf. Psalm 139:21f) is nowhere to be found in Scripture. Though this is true literally, Jesus puts his finger here on the eternal human tendency to separate people into two classes and to act in consequence. There are those who are with me ("my neighbors"), and then there are the others ("my enemies"). Even Israel's calling to be a "kingdom of priests" for the whole of humanity was unable fully to check this tendency.

In the Sermon on the Mount, Jesus explains the commandment in a way that eliminates all possible ambiguity:

> *You have heard that it was said:* You shall love your neighbor *and hate your enemy. But I say to you: Love your enemies and pray for those who persecute you, so that you may be children of your Father in heaven, for he causes his sun to rise on the evil and the good, and makes rain fall on those who do right and those who do wrong. For if you love those who love you, what reward will you receive? Do not tax-collectors act the same way? And if you greet only your brothers and sisters, what are you doing that is so special? Do not Gentiles do the same thing? You for your part must be perfect, as your heavenly Father is perfect.* (Matthew 5:43-48)

Believers are called to imitate the behavior of their God, and Jesus states unequivocally that, unlike human beings, God is an enemy to nobody. The newness of the Gospel consists less in belief in a God whose love is all-inclusive[12] (cf. Isaiah 55:7-9), than in the conviction that, following in the steps of Jesus, human beings are capable of a nonjudgmental concern for the other, whoever he or she may be.

This concern is shown even more dramatically in the well-known parable of the Good Samaritan (Luke 10:25-37). After evoking the twofold commandment of love, the expert in the Torah pushes Jesus further by asking him the question "And who is my neighbor?" Instead of giving an abstract answer by naming a specific group of people, Jesus tells a story. An abstract answer, incidentally, would have been particularly inappropriate in such a discussion. "My neighbor" refers to the woman or man I am called to show love to in a given context by the way I act. Such love, by its nature, cannot be extended to a whole category of people, not even to "all humanity," but only to concrete individuals, one by one. Jesus' choice to respond by telling a parable thus already provides a preliminary answer to the question of the identity of my neighbor: he leaves behind the clouds of abstraction and brings the discussion down to earth by descending from the theoretical to the practical level.

Jesus tells a story of three men on their way to Jerusalem who have an identical experience. On the road they find someone half-dead, the victim of bandits. Two clergymen pass by, presumably in order not to compromise their ritual purity. The third, a Samaritan, stops and offers all the aid necessary, showing extraordinary generosity. In his question to the expert after telling the story, Jesus accomplishes another highly significant reversal: "Who shows himself to be (*genonenai*) a neighbor to the man who fell into the hands of robbers?" (Luke 10:36). For Jesus, the essential is not to divide humanity into an in-group and an out-group, "my neighbors" and the others, but rather to *behave* as a neighbor to whoever crosses my path. The first step is not some act of intellectual discrimination to determine if the person I come into contact with fits into the prescribed class of people, whether it be religious, social, economic or other, but a readiness to let my heart be touched by the needs that arise out of the situation I am confronted with, to respond as a neighbor to the person who stands in front of me. I am called to be available to be a neighbor to anyone and everyone, in particular to the one who needs my help in the present moment.

TO THE ENDS OF THE EARTH

Rooting himself in the great tradition of the centuries-long relationship between Israel and its God, Jesus was thus the bringer of a new outlook that carried "the Law and the Prophets" to their fulfillment (see Matthew 5:17). In him, the long-awaited and definitive Reign of God has broken into the world here below, albeit in an enigmatic and unexpected way, unfathomable to those without the eyes to see (cf. Mark 4:10-12, 8:14-21). In the domain of interpersonal relations, we have seen that the inbreaking of God's Reign involves both a closer relationship between love of God and love of neighbor, and a widening of the category of "neighbor" to the extreme. This new teaching of Jesus could not fail to have far-reaching consequences for the way his disciples envisaged the community to which they belonged.

Basically, the New Testament tells the story of the evolution of Christianity from a movement within the Jewish people to a worldwide and all-inclusive phenomenon. It has become common to describe this evolution as the birth of a "new religion," but we have already seen that the notion of "religion" is not the most helpful category for understanding what is distinctive about the Christian faith. The key development seems rather to be a shift in the reference group for those who became followers of Jesus. This shift did not happen overnight, but when it did, it was radical and unprecedented, finding its sole justification in the belief that, in fact, a new age in human history was dawning. Since we are probably too used to this aspect of Christianity to be aware of its radical newness, it is important to draw it out in some detail.

We must begin by recalling yet again that the people of Israel drew their identity first and foremost not from ethnic or geographical factors, but from a common relationship to the God who called their ancestors out of slavery to freedom and gave them a land of their own. This divine call, moreover, was never intended as a kind of privilege for a restricted group; if Israel was thus "set apart" (Numbers 23:9), it was in order to be a "kingdom of priests and a holy nation" (Exodus 19:6), that is, a sign of God's presence for the entire world. And in an indeterminate future, that presence would bear fruit beyond measure: the prophets of Israel had premonitions of a time to come when all the nations of the earth would recognize the One God as the Source of their life and thus be drawn into an association with God's people:

> *At the end of days, the mountain of the Lord's house will be established as the chief among the mountains and be lifted up above the*

hills. And all nations will stream to it. Many peoples will come and say: Come, let us go up to the mountain of the Lord, to the house of the God of Jacob. He will teach us his ways and we shall walk in his paths. For instruction will go forth from Zion and the Lord's Word from Jerusalem. (…) Thus says the Lord of hosts: Nations and the inhabitants of great cities will again come in, and dwellers in one will say to another: Let us go before the Lord to entreat him and to seek the Lord of hosts; I am going too. Many peoples and mighty nations will go to seek the Lord of hosts in Jerusalem and to entreat him. Thus says the Lord of hosts: In those days ten men speaking all the tongues of the nations will take hold of a Jew by his garment and say: We want to go with you, for we have heard that God is with you. (Isaiah 2:2-3; Zechariah 8:20-23)

A universal outlook was thus implicitly part and parcel of biblical faith virtually from the outset. In practice, however, for most of its history Israel was defined by ethnic and political criteria; it was seen—even by itself—as one nation among others. There was, to be sure, always a degree of osmosis with neighboring peoples. Resident aliens, foreigners joined by marriage, and, later, proselytes and sympathizers (so-called godfearers) allied with those born into the Jewish people. But these were essentially marginal phenomena, and there was no explicit call to undertake any positive action to widen the frontiers of the chosen people.

In the wake of Jesus of Nazareth, this situation underwent a radical transformation. His life and teaching ultimately broke down all the barriers that separated human beings; in him, God reached out and called to fellowship whoever crossed his path.[13] This soon gave rise to thorny questions. What should be done about the non-Jews who were attracted to the person and message of Jesus? Should they first be integrated into the chosen people before being accepted into full fellowship with the followers of Christ? If not, what did this mean for the Jewish disciples of Jesus and their own religious affiliation? Since satisfactory answers to these questions were far from obvious, it is no surprise that it took some time for the members of the "Jesus movement" to see their way clearly in this regard.

It is the second part of Luke's story of Christian origins, the book we call The Acts of the Apostles, which deals most exhaustively with this evolution. In it we see that, independently of the will of the early Christians and indeed most often in opposition to their conscious intent, the Gospel constantly expanded both geographically and sociologically. It traveled from "Jerusalem to all of Judea and Samaria, and to the ends of the earth" (Acts 1:8), which for Luke meant essentially Rome, the capital of the empire from which a new beginning would be possible. At the same time, the beneficiaries of the message were extended from Palestinian Aramaic-speaking Jews, to Greek-speaking Jews, to Samaritans and godfearers, and finally to Gentiles of all stripes, since "God shows no partiality, but in all nations, whoever honors him and acts rightly is acceptable to him" (Acts 10:34f).

What is perhaps most striking about this expansion is its spontaneous and unreflective character. The disciples are moved, not by deliberation and decision, but by the pressure of events that are often in themselves negative. By emphasizing this aspect, Luke certainly wants to indicate that not human calculation but God's Spirit[14] is the moving force behind the spread of the Gospel. As is shown most saliently in the crucifixion of Jesus (cf. Acts 2:23f),

God has the ability to bring a greater good out of human evil.

Thus, it is on account of a "great persecution" in Jerusalem following the martyrdom of Stephen that the disciples are dispersed throughout Judea and Samaria (Acts 8:1). The deacon Philip seizes the occasion to "proclaim the Christ" in Samaria and win converts there. Shortly thereafter, he is inspired to encounter an Ethiopian government official, a sympathizer with the Jewish religion, and make him a disciple of Jesus (chap. 8). These small steps for the Gospel outside Israel are the prelude to the main event, recounted in chapters 10 and 11, for which the apostle Peter is the protagonist.

Peter undertakes to visit the different groups of believers throughout the region (Acts 9:32). In Joppa, he has a vision that is extremely shocking for a practicing Jew like him: he is told to disobey the laws of kosher and eat animals considered unclean. This vision soon brings him to the house of the Roman centurion Cornelius, a godfearer who in his turn has had a vision announcing Peter's visit. Peter is thus led to proclaim the Good News to these Gentiles, who immediately experience the power of the Holy Spirit and are then baptized. When he returns to Jerusalem, he must explain his unusual behavior before the community, who finally reaches the conviction that God has indeed opened a new door:

> *Peter said, "If God has given them the same gift he gave to us when we believed in the Lord Jesus Christ, who was I to set up obstacles to God?" When they heard this they were silenced and gave glory to God, saying, "So God has given to the Gentiles too the change of heart that leads to Life!"* (Acts 11:17f)

From then on, non-Jews have the right to hear and to respond to the Christian message just as well as Jews. The point man for this endeavor, however, is not Peter but Paul, the former Pharisee and persecutor of Christians who was called by God "to bear [Christ's] Name before the Gentiles, before kings and the children of Israel" (Acts 9:15). It is true that Paul, as well, initially intends to proclaim the Good News to the Jews, but in the face of their refusal he turns to the Gentiles:

> *Speaking out boldly, Paul and Barnabas declared: "We were required to speak the Word of God first of all to you! Since you refuse to accept it and do not consider yourselves worthy of eternal life, we are turning towards the Gentiles. For this is what the Lord ordered us to do: 'I have appointed you a light to the nations, so that you may bring salvation to the ends of the earth.'"* (Acts 13:46f; cf. Acts 18:5f, 28:23-28)

Once again, a seeming hindrance reveals itself to be providential for the progress of the Gospel.

The game is not yet over, however. The decision to allow non-Jews to become full-fledged disciples of Jesus without first becoming members of the Jewish people is so revolutionary that it requires a formal ratification by the Christian leadership. This is recounted in chapter 15 of Acts and is often known as the Council or Assembly of Jerusalem. Luke reports the interventions of Peter and James, representing two different tendencies, which nonetheless have the same basic premise in common. In their closing letter, the apostles use this bold phrase: "The Holy Spirit and we have resolved not to impose on you any more burdens than what is necessary" (Acts 15:28). This formula is not an attempt to arrogate authority to oneself by speaking in God's name, but precisely the opposite: the recognition that God's Spirit often leads human beings in a direction where they never imagined they would go.

From then on, despite momentary setbacks, the way is open for the Gospel to set out from Palestine and Asia Minor, cross over into Europe (Acts 16:9f), reach Athens (Acts 17:15ff), Corinth (Acts 18:1ff), and finally Rome. The coming of the Christian message to Rome is also portrayed by Luke as a result of chance events that are, in fact, signs of divine intervention. When forced to appear before a Roman tribunal in Palestine, as a Roman citizen Paul exercises his right to appeal to the emperor (Acts 25:11f). This requires a long trip to the capital, one that is humanly speaking unnecessary, since the king and the governor have already judged him innocent (Acts 26:30-32). And the road to Rome is beset with a whole series of hardships. But in the middle of a tempest, the apostle is assured by a divine messenger: "Do not be afraid, Paul. It is necessary for you to appear before the emperor, and so God grants you the safety of all your fellow-travelers" (Acts 27:24). Once again, it is God who is in charge of events, even making use of resistances and obstacles so that, in the end, from the center of the *oikoumenē*, the inhabited earth, the proclamation of God's Reign and the teaching of Jesus may go out "freely and without hindrance" (Acts 28:31). Despite the relatively small number of its adherents, Christianity is already in essence a worldwide reality.

CITIZENS AND YET FOREIGNERS

The unique character of the teaching of Jesus of Nazareth thus gave rise to a new form of interpersonal relations, superficially similar to but ultimately unlike any other human group. Like the Torah of Israel, this teaching was, by its nature, creative of community. The fact that believers saw themselves as members of the same family, God's family, was not only incidental to their faith but rather an essential expression of it. In this sense, the early church differed from the other religious associations that were springing up in the Roman Empire at the beginning of the Common Era. On the other hand, unlike Israel, for Christians, ethnic and political bonds never defined their common belonging. The universal appeal of their faith was thus more clearly apparent to all.

It cannot be denied that a series of external, historical factors contributed greatly to the success of the new movement. Something so new in human terms required the right conditions to come into being. From a theological point of view, it would not be wrong to speak of the working of divine providence. In any case, it is clear that even in its social structure, the Christian faith was a fully incarnational phenomenon, defining itself in interaction with contemporary historical realities.

The first of these was the *pax romana*, which began in the years just before the birth of Jesus and lasted for centuries. The entire Mediterranean world was unified under a common government, which nonetheless respected local customs insofar as they did not call Roman hegemony into question. Moreover, the fact that Israel had not been an independent state for centuries favored the dissemination of Judaism throughout the empire. Most Jews lived in a situation of diaspora, which gave the institution of the synagogue an importance it never had in Palestine, where the temple was easily accessible. The social structure of the Jewish people at the time, that of an international network of communities with no political independence, offered an obvious model to the burgeoning "Jesus movement." And when, as a result of the Jewish wars of 70, 115, and 135 CE, nationalistic elements within the Jewish world came to the fore and contributed to a loss of prestige of that faith within the empire, the Christians were there to keep alive, and to profit from, the universalistic heritage of Judaism.

At the same time, the decadence of the old Greco-Roman paganism and the awakening of widespread spiritual anxiety favored openness to new religious ideas, notably cults coming from the East. The Christian faith fit without too much trouble into this category of religions of personal salvation, at least at first glance, and possessed the additional advantage of being rooted in the age-old reality of Israel. It thus brought together, in a unique way, ancient wisdom and an up-to-date response to spiritual searching. Likewise, with its spirituality of being "in the world but not of the world," it occupied a middle ground between total and suicidal rejection of the surrounding society, on the one hand, and complete assimilation, which would have caused it to lose its unique identity, on the other. And finally, by its emphasis on intense community life, it brought together the religious and social dimensions of existence more effectively than many of its competitors.[15]

The spirit of Jesus, which for Christians is in fact the Spirit of God continuing the work of creation, thus gradually brought about in the world an unprecedented form of social belonging.

It could be variously described as a people, yet one not based on ethnic or geographical bonds and holding no political power, or as a family, but a worldwide one with God at its head. Or, again, it could be compared with the human body and its many parts but in a way that went far beyond a metaphor, since this body was the Body of Christ himself, in other words, his ongoing real presence in human history (see pp. 28ff). Such a description of the "Christian commonwealth" according to the logic of "similar but in fact different" is shown most clearly in an extraordinary text from the early Christian centuries, known as the *Letter to Diognetus:*

> *Christians cannot be distinguished from the rest of the human race by country or language or customs. They do not live in cities of their own; they do not use a peculiar form of speech; they do not follow an eccentric manner of life. This doctrine of theirs has not been discovered by the ingenuity or deep thought of inquisitive men, nor do they put forward a merely human teaching, as some people do. Yet, although they live in Greek and barbarian cities alike, as each man's lot has been cast, and follow the customs of the country in clothing and food and other matters of daily living, at the same time they give proof of the remarkable and admittedly extraordinary constitution of their own commonwealth. They live in their own countries, but only as aliens. They have a share in everything as citizens, and endure everything as foreigners. Every foreign land is their fatherland, and yet for them every fatherland is a foreign land. They marry, like everyone else, and they beget children, but they do not cast out their offspring. They share their board with each other, but not their marriage*

*bed. It is true that they are "in the flesh," but they do not live
"according to the flesh." They busy themselves on earth, but their
citizenship is in heaven. They obey the established laws, but in
their own lives they go far beyond what the laws require. They
love all men, and by all men are persecuted. They are unknown,
and still they are condemned; they are put to death, and yet they
are brought to life. They are poor, and yet they make many rich;
they are completely destitute, and yet they enjoy complete abundance. They are dishonored, and in their very dishonor are glori-
fied; they are defamed, and are vindicated. They are reviled, and
yet they bless; when they are affronted, they still pay due respect.
When they do good, they are punished as evildoers; undergoing
punishment, they rejoice because they are brought to life. They
are treated by the Jews as foreigners and enemies, and are hunted
down by the Greeks; and all the time those who hate them find it
impossible to justify their enmity.* (5:1-17)

The anonymous author concludes with his own preferred image:
"What the soul is in the body, that Christians are in the world"
(*Letter to Diognetus* 6:1), fundamentally different from yet insepa-
rably attached to human society.

A CATHOLIC COMMUNITY

The term eventually chosen by the disciples of Jesus to describe
their own life together was the Greek word *ekklēsia*, which passed
through Latin to become *église, chiesa, iglesia, igreja* in the Ro-
mance languages.[16] The original meaning of the word, from the
etymology "those called out," refers to an official convocation of

people to deliberate and to make laws, notably to the assembly of citizens in the Greek city-states. In the Greek version of the Hebrew Scriptures, it was used to translate the Hebrew word *qahal*, the assembly of Israel called together by God, primarily for worship (e.g., Deuteronomy 31:30; 1 Kings 8:14, 22, 55). The term thus emphasizes that what unites believers is a common call from God and describes less a static "institution" with its permanent structures than a dynamic reality, a "congregation" brought together to accomplish a specific task, to be a visible sign or icon of God's presence at the heart of human history.

Although the term *ekklēsia* signifies, first and foremost, that we are called out, and called together, by God, in practice things are a bit more complex. If the community of believers has sign value, that means that God's call takes place in large part through the mediation of human beings. Practically speaking, Christians generally come to Christ as a result of the Christians who have gone before them (cf. John 1:41-42, 45-46, 4:28-30). They experience divine love and forgiveness through the witness of committed believers; they learn about the Gospel and deepen their understanding of it thanks to Christian parents and teachers; they are incorporated into the faith community by receiving the sacraments celebrated by Christian ministers. In practice, therefore, the church is both the fellowship called together by Christ and the fellowship by means of which Christ calls others. Here we see another consequence of the incarnate nature of the Christian faith; no hard-and-fast distinction can be drawn between the working of God and the activity of human beings transformed by God's Spirit, since the two are not on the same level. God brings more and more people into communion by means of those who have already responded to his call and attempt to make it a reality in their lives.[17]

The Christian community, the church, is a unique form of human togetherness in another way also. Its various local manifestations are not parts of a whole, pieces of a puzzle, but rather potentially full and authentic expressions of that whole. To return to the image of the body, when the Christian church in each locality is gathered around its pastor—and this occurs paradigmatically in the celebration of the Eucharist—not turned in upon itself but in communion with all the other churches, it does not represent a part of the body such as the arm or the foot; it is rather the whole body in microcosm. If we want to keep the image of the human body, a helpful analogy might be this: each local church is like a cell containing within itself all the genes that could be used, should the occasion arise, as a blueprint to regenerate the entire body. Or more simply, we can think of the same sun reflected in a multitude of raindrops. Each local community is the whole church made present in a particular place, always provided that it remains in living fellowship with all those who profess one and the same faith.

The term traditionally used to express this unique quality of the Christian church is the word *catholic*. Unfortunately, today this term is understood either as the name of one part of the Christian people, namely, the churches in full communion with the bishop of Rome, or else as referring to the geographical universality of Christianity, spread across the world. Despite a widespread misconception, however, the word *catholic* is not simply a synonym for worldwide or universal. The church is called catholic, from the Greek expression *kath'holou*, "according to the whole," first and foremost because in its very constitution it is the opposite of a sect. However small or limited the concrete manifestation of a particular community is, in it Christ is present, and thus all human divisions and barriers are transcended; it is the efficacious sign of a unity that reconciles all diversity in a common belonging. Once again, it is, above all, in the celebration of the Eucharist that this sign becomes fully manifest. The geographical expansion of Christianity is only one of the external and visible consequences of this intrinsic quality of every true Christian community: because it makes Christ present, the One in whom creation is brought into oneness with God and therefore into unity within itself, it tends toward all-inclusiveness by its very nature.[18]

At the same time, like every incarnational reality of faith, the Christian church suffers from a gap between its essential identity and its empirical appearance. Over the course of centuries, it has inevitably been affected by the vagaries of history. Its historical manifestation has moved along a continuum marked by two extremes, either of which, if it became exclusive, would ring the death knell of its unique character. At certain periods, when it became successful in human terms and enjoyed the approval of the rulers of the wider society, Christianity ran the risk of becoming the official religion of a secular state. In such a case, the distinction between the church and civil society is blurred, and so the sign value of the Christian community, in obedience to its call to mirror the Absolute of God in the midst of human history, becomes seriously impaired.

At such moments, a salutary reaction inevitably arose from the embers of a faith become, to a great extent, conformity to the world. Individuals and groups rediscovered the prophetic character of the Christian message, its call to a newness of life fundamentally different from the values of a society based on violence and greed, and acted in consequence. Returning to the roots of biblical faith, they reenacted in their own existence the response of their ancestor Abraham to the call from God: "Leave your home and family for the land I will show you" (Genesis 12:1). Sometimes this exodus was a geographical one, as when those known as the Desert Fathers and Mothers left the cities of Egypt in the fourth century to live in the wilderness. At other times, believers continued to live in the midst of society but ratified their separation by a distinctive lifestyle, thus returning in a certain sense to the example of the early Christian communities.

Despite the fact that the original impulse for these groups was often authentically evangelical, namely, the perception that faith in Jesus involved leaving the "wide and spacious road that leads to ruin" for the "narrow road and gate that leads to life" (Matthew 7:13-14), their existence was not without its own problems. The Christian communities we encounter in the New Testament, although small in number and influence, had a universal outlook implicitly present in the Gospel they professed. They were bearers of an unlimited communion, mustard seeds on their way to growing into a large plant. Groups within the Christian world that rediscovered the radical call of the Gospel later on followed a different trajectory, however. They often tended to split off from the wider church, either by conscious choice or by the incomprehension and rejection of the parent body or, more commonly, by a combination of the two. They therefore ran the risk of incorporating into their identity an element of refusal, of defining themselves over *against* other believers in Christ. The accent could then imperceptibly shift from being a sign of universal communion in God to considering oneself as the remnant of true believers surrounded by a hostile world. A defensive, sectarian attitude could then begin to make itself felt or, at the very least, a justification of divisions on the basis of a certain doctrinal purity.

Here, too, authentic faith eventually led to healthy reactions. The ecumenical movement of the twentieth century is a striking example of this. Christians began to feel more and more deeply that the situation of division among themselves, which they had taken for granted for centuries, was, in fact, the most telling argument against the truth of their claims. How could believers in a God of love, who called all humans to an intimate relationship made concrete in an all-inclusive belonging, justify, in good conscience, mutual excommunications in the name of their founder? "May they be one so that the world may believe" (John 17:21): these words of Jesus just before his death definitively eliminate any facile justification of denominational separations among his followers, if they are to be true to their mission.

Examining the two extreme positions that call into question the unique character of the Christian community at least possesses the advantage of pointing us in the right direction, even if it provides no infallible path for getting there. It delineates the task that lies before us. Can we imagine a church that maintains a critical distance from the powers of this world without neglecting the welfare of the entire human community? One that cultivates intense relationships of fellowship among its members while at the same time being open to all? One that, although offering a Gospel alternative to the values of the wider society, does not view itself self-righteously as a small group of the pure? A church that, in short, is neither a sect nor an apologist for the Establishment, but the place where the leaven of the Gospel attempts to penetrate the human dough in all its opacity, where an all-inclusive love of neighbor becomes a tangible rule of life? In order to suggest a possible answer to these questions, we must first turn to a consideration of the topic of friendship.

3

Friendship

If divine love lies at the heart of the Christian faith, and if this love takes concrete shape in the constitution of a community where we love one another as God has loved us, then it is imperative to investigate more deeply the characteristics of this love. The word "love" is multifaceted; it covers a host of exceedingly diverse situations. We love God, our mother, our cat, football, and pizza. In his much-celebrated study on the subject, the well-known Christian thinker and writer C. S. Lewis distinguished four different kinds of love: *storgē* or affection, *philia* or friendship, *eros* or desire, and *agapē* or charity.[19] Of the first three, he considered friendship the least "natural," meaning by this that it did not fill as clearly as the others did an innate need of the human animal and thus had a stronger rational or spiritual component. Interestingly, he felt that it was precisely this "spiritual" quality of friendship that rendered it less apt to express realities of the faith: it was too close to the latter while at the same time being distinct from them, thus creating possible confusion.

Nonetheless, even Lewis conceded that companionship was "the matrix of friendship,"[20] and indeed it would not be wrong to situate the roots of what we call friendship in the gregarious nature of human life. "It is not good for the *adam* to be alone," says God at the beginning of the Bible (Genesis 2:18). If, in fact, we are created to live in society with others of our kind, friendship can be seen as a particularly explicit form of this life with others. What was especially characteristic of friendship, according to Lewis, was its rootedness in the discovery by two people of a common interest that went beyond their own persons. He expresses this succinctly by contrasting it with *eros*: "Lovers are always talking to one another about their love; Friends hardly ever about their Friendship. Lovers are normally face to face; Friends, side by side, absorbed in some common interest."[21] Friendship must be *about* something; it is not interested in the other *qua* other. In this respect Lewis was strongly, and quite understandably, influenced by his own experience. What he considered his oldest and truest friendship, one with a certain Arthur Greeves, was based on a mutual fascination with myth and fantasy; in other domains the two had much less in common. And later on, his vision of friendship expressed itself emblematically in the creation of the Inklings, an informal group that met weekly in an Oxford pub to read the members' writings and discuss related topics.

One has the impression that Lewis' understanding of friendship is a bit idiosyncratic; not all would agree that the image of two individuals with a common pastime or hobby is the best way of describing friends. Are not most people interested in the *person* of their friend as much as in the interests shared in common, to a greater degree than the Oxford don would admit? Certainly Lewis's own life would seem to corroborate this. Yet with that caveat, he does put his finger on a defining characteristic of the love of friends that makes it particularly interesting for our purposes. He shares it with none other than the great Greek philosopher Aristotle, for whom friendship is based on *koina*, things held in common, or *koinōnia*, a commonality of interests, a sharing of something. Friendship by this account is eminently *triadic*, and so corresponds exceptionally well to the biblical understanding of the essence of human relations.[22]

FRIENDSHIP THROUGH THE AGES

In the ancient world, friendship was aristocratic and occasionally cosmic.[23] The classical Roman writer Cicero wrote an influential work on the subject, having in mind ideal relationships between well-off citizens, based not on need or profit but cultivated for their own sake. A friend was an *alter ego*, another self, with whom one could find pleasure of the mind in sharing the most intimate things. A defining characteristic of such relationships was loyalty or faithfulness (*fides*), and the investment of time and energy required seemed to preclude a too-wide extension of the circle. On a more theoretical and indeed utopian level, which one may regard in some sense as an anticipation of the Christian outlook, the Stoic philosophers envisaged the ideal society as a "friendship of the wise." Earlier, the Greek philosopher Empedocles had spoken of *philia* as a "force, both physical and moral, that binds and creates harmony throughout the universe."[24] These two visions of friendship, the personal, on the one hand, and the social or cosmic, on the other, never seem to have been brought into explicit harmony by the ancients, and there was little or no investigation into the roots of friendship, in other words the kind of love that made it possible. It was Christianity that would come to fill in the gaps, both deepening and widening the pagan understanding of the notion.

This is not to say that the theme of friendship plays a preponderant role in the New Testament. To indicate the relationship between believers, it is far outstripped by other images. And yet the human reality of friendship plays a part in the world of the Gospel, particularly in the Lucan writings (e.g., Luke 11:5, 15:6; Acts 10:24). Jesus himself is described as a "friend of tax-collectors and sinners" (Matthew 11:19), and John's Gospel speaks of his particular attachment to Lazarus and his sisters (John 11:3, 36; cf. John 11:5, *ēgapa*). The fourth evangelist, for his part, occasionally uses the verb *phileō*, friendship-love, as an alternative to *agapaō*, Christian love or charity. On two occasions, Jesus refers to his disciples as his friends (John 15:12-15; Luke 12:4), and in the third letter of John "the friends" seems to be a designation of believers, replacing the more normal "the brothers (and sisters)" (3 John 15). While the notion is not exclusively used for Christians—one can be a friend of the world (James 4:4; cf. John 15:19) or of the emperor (John 19:12)—the language of friendship fleshes out the reality of Christian love, helping to anchor it in our existence here on earth.

As was the case for many other topics, making use of the language of friendship to elucidate the Gospel of Jesus Christ led to an evolution in the notion itself. For Christians, the "thing in common" that made them friends was not a human attribute but the common experience of being called by Christ to be a follower of his. Friendship could thus be applied to an essentially unequal relationship, that between Christ, or even God, and believers. In addition, this friendship was potentially universal, since all are called to discipleship. The Christian outlook thus radically contradicted one aspect of friendship as it was heretofore understood: its exclusive or restricted character.

Augustine

We have a prototypic example of the transition between the classical and Christian understandings of friendship in the life of the thinker of late antiquity who perhaps more than anyone else, for better and for worse, gave shape to Western Christianity for centuries to come, Augustine of Hippo (354-430).[25] By temperament, background, and training, Saint Augustine was particularly disposed to accord great importance to friendship. For him, life without the company of other like-minded people was hardly worth living. In his *Confessions*, he speaks movingly of the joys friendship held for him as a young man:

> *to talk and laugh together and good-naturedly give into one another by turns; to read entertaining books together; to joke and be serious together; to get into arguments without animosity just as a person argues with himself, and by these rare disagreements to add spice to the agreement in practically everything; to teach things to each other and to learn from each other; to pine for those absent and to welcome with gladness those who arrive. These and other similar signs proceeding from the heart of those who love and are loved in return, through the mouth, the tongue, the eyes and a thousand kindly gestures, are like tinder that sets souls on fire and makes one out of many.* (*Confessions*, IV, 8)

This passage comes immediately after Augustine tells of the premature death of a close friend of his youth, someone to whom he was so attached that as a result, he fell into a deep and long-lasting depression:

> *The pain [of his death] plunged my heart into darkness; wherever I looked I saw only death. My native land was torture and my father's home deep unhappiness, and whatever I had shared with him, without him was changed into the utmost torment. (…) Only my tears were sweet to me; they took the place of my friend as the joy of my soul. (…) For I felt that my soul and his soul were one soul in two bodies, and therefore life was a horror for me, because I did not want to live cut in half. (Confessions, IV, 4.6)*

Characteristically, it was the presence of other friends in his life that eventually healed the wound.

At that time, Augustine was not yet a Christian. In his search for spiritual truth or "wisdom," as he put it, he attracted a group of like-minded individuals around him, one of whom was his mother Monica, although she was already a believer in Christ. A topic of conversation that continually came up was the prospect of their all going off together to lead a common life, away from the bustle and distractions of life in society:

> *A number of us friends had been thinking and speaking together about something. Detesting the turbulent troubles of human life, we had just about determined to go off and live a life of leisure far from the crowds, and to organize our leisure so that if we possessed anything, we would put it in common and all of us come*

together to form a single household. In that way, in the purity of friendship, nothing would belong to one more than to another, but everything would be one, everything for each and all for all. There were about ten of us who thought we could be part of this company. . . . We thought it a very good idea for two of us to take turns as managers every year to look after all the necessities, so that the others could be left undisturbed. But later on, when we began to consider whether the women would accept this—for some of us had wives and the rest of us were desirous of marrying— everything we had resolved and conceived so well fell into pieces in our hands and was broken up and cast aside. (*Confessions*, VI, 14)

Although this project came to nothing, later on, on the eve of his conversion, Augustine retired with his mother and a few friends to a country house outside Milan, at Cassiciacum, during his vacation from teaching (*Confessions*, IX, 4). And upon his return to Africa, his longtime dream of a group of friends living together in spiritual and material sharing took shape in a cenobitic[26] community for which he eventually wrote a rule of life. Later on, as priest and bishop, he continued to live in community with other committed men. It is significant that what attracted Augustine to the monastic tradition was not primarily, as for the desert fathers and mothers of Egypt, the desire for solitude, but rather a concrete way of sharing life along the lines of the early Christian community as shown in the Acts of the Apostles.

Augustine's life as a Christian and a bishop thus represented a deepening, or even better a transfiguration, of his natural penchant for companionship and conversation with others, for life together. Looking back over his past in his *Confessions*, he sees the limits of his earlier outlook. He now estimates that the friend of his youth was not a true friend, since, as he expresses to God,

> *there is no true friendship unless you bind together those who are attached to you by the charity "poured into our hearts through the Holy Spirit, who is given to us." [Romans 5:5] (...) Happy those who love you, and their friend in you, and their enemy because of you.* (*Confessions*, IV, 4.9)

Friends in Christ thus have God as the bond between them or, more precisely, that divine love, which is God's own breath of life, or Spirit.

Writing to an old friend, Marcianus, who is in the process of becoming a Christian, Augustine takes up Cicero's definition of friendship and applies it to their new situation:

> *You know of course how the man someone called the most eloquent Roman author of all defined friendship. He said, and spoke very truly, that* Friendship is an agreement on matters human and divine, with goodwill and affection. *(...) Our friendship was defective; it was only an agreement on human and not divine matters, though with goodwill and affection. (...) But now, how can I find the words to tell you how happy I am that I have as a true friend someone who in a certain sense has already been my friend for a long time? We are now in agreement concerning the things of God. (...) I thank God for making you my friend at last. For now we have* agreement on matters human and divine, with goodwill and affection *in Christ Jesus our Lord, our true peace. He summed up all his teachings in two precepts,*

saying: You shall love the Lord your God with your whole heart, your whole soul and your whole mind and: You shall love your neighbor as yourself. On these two commandments depend the whole Law and the Prophets. *The first deals with divine matters, the second with human ones. (...) If we keep both firmly, our friendship will be true and everlasting, and will not only unite us to each other but also to the Lord himself.* (Letter no. 258)

For Augustine, too, Christian friendship is potentially universal. Since true love means wishing well to others, it extends to all, even to our enemies. And yet, because of the circumstances of life on earth, we cannot show friendship to all concretely. When love is reciprocal and rooted in God's love communicated to us in Christ, it truly merits the name of friendship. In heaven, this will finally be the case.[27]

Significantly and perhaps surprisingly, the most perfect image of friendship for Augustine comes at the end of the narrative part of his *Confessions*. He describes a conversation he had at Ostia with his mother Monica shortly before her death. Mother and son, avidly conversing about the things of God, are gradually lifted up into the heavenly realms and together touch for a brief moment "the region of inexhaustible fullness, where you nourish Israel for ever with the food of truth, and where life is the Wisdom by which all things were made" (*Confessions*, IX, 10). We are shown the portrait of a deep affection between two human beings that both results from, and opens the way to, communion with the wellspring of all life. The triadic nature of Christian love could scarcely be expressed any better.

If the life of Saint Augustine illustrates admirably the transfiguration of friendship because of Christ, it must nonetheless be added that Augustine's own comprehension of this was out of phase with his life. When he writes specifically as a theologian, one is struck by the limited role that human friendship plays in his thought. He is far from having perceived all the resonances of this topic. There are at least two reasons for this. The first is that, as a convert to Christianity, Augustine viewed his life as sharply divided into a "before" and an "after," with the "before" clearly given a negative value, because of the inevitable contrast with the new state of affairs. We can be sure that he would have subscribed fully to the feelings of his mentor, Saint Paul, writing about his own past: "All these things which were an advantage for me, I have considered a loss on account of Christ. (...) Because of him I have lost everything and consider it rubbish, so that I might acquire Christ" (Philippians 3:7-8). This tendency on the part of those who have undergone a radical change of life to consider their past existence "rubbish" means that even things good in themselves, such as human affection and desires, tend to be seen in a negative light; the better makes the good seem bad.

This psychological reason was reinforced by a philosophical one. Augustine was strongly influenced by a neo-Platonic philosophy, which considered human life as a pilgrimage upwards to union with the divine. In this way of thinking, earthly goods are transitional, a mere shadow of what is real; the important thing is for the soul to go beyond them to attain the one true reality, the source of all being. This philosophy, for all its grandeur, did not succeed in giving full weight to the incarnate dimension of the Christian Gospel, to the presence of the Most

High God squarely in the midst of the human condition: "The Word became flesh, and dwelt among us" (John 1:14). Much of Augustine's thinking and writing was thus an attempt to express the Gospel, in which he so deeply believed and so authentically practiced, in a philosophical language in some ways antipathetic to its basic orientation.

Augustine thus did not have either the psychological makeup or the conceptual tools to understand fully what his heart found so important and to integrate it into his vision of the faith. Alongside a conviction that the "one heart and soul" of those united by Christian love truly fulfills on earth the intention of God,[28] there remains in him a nagging fear that the joys of human friendship may draw one's heart away from the one thing that matters. We have already seen how distraught he was at the death of his childhood friend. When, many years later, now a Christian, he loses the person who was, in fact, closest to him, his mother Monica, significantly he reproaches himself for feeling grief at the loss, as if that implied doubting eternal life or according more love to a creature than to the Creator:

> *Because I was bereft of such a great consolation in her, my soul was wounded and my life, which had been made one between me and her, almost torn into pieces. (...) And since I was deeply annoyed that these human feelings, which because of the natural order and our human condition must of necessity arise, had so much power over me, I suffered an additional suffering in addition to my suffering and was tormented by a double sadness. (...) And if someone finds that I have sinned because I wept for my mother for part of an hour, (...) let him not laugh, but rather, if he is a*

charitable person, let him weep for my sins before you, the Father of all the brothers of your Christ. (*Confessions*, IX, 12)

Although this "dramatic" mode of existence was undoubtedly one of the secrets of Augustine's vitality and explains the great influence he has had on so many people down through the ages, at times one cannot help but wish that such a seminal figure for Western Christianity could have achieved greater serenity by reconciling in himself the claims of God and the realities of the human condition. The question is complex, and indeed can never be resolved adequately, since the world as we know it is undeniably marked by sin. In other words, there is inevitably both continuity and a clear break between the human condition as it is, on the one hand, and as God wishes it to be, on the other; no facile accord between the human and the divine is possible that does not pass through the Cross. And yet, for believers, the Cross is ultimately the shadow side of the Resurrection, and in the light of Christ's paradoxical victory over evil, the last word infallibly belongs to reconciliation. Is not the impression, whether justified or not, that sin rather than divine *philanthropia* (see Titus 3:4) lies at the heart of the Christian faith one of the reasons why so many of our contemporaries look askance at that faith? The challenge for later theology will be to integrate the "either-or" of Augustine into a fully incarnational outlook that gives full weight to the importance of human realities. Rather than placing God in opposition to God's creation, such a theology should show how created realities can become an authentic "parable" of the divine, offering a foretaste of heaven. The same Jesus who said "whoever is not with me is against me" (Matthew 12:30) also stated "whoever is not against us is for us" (Mark 9:40), and Saint Paul reminds us that "to the pure all things are pure" (Titus 1:15). In the topic that interests us here, there is an urgent need to elaborate a vision of friendship that views friendship in Christ not as an alternative to but as a deepening or more exactly a transfiguration of human affection, where in the end nothing is lost. The story of Saint Augustine's life, more than his thought, offers precious indications in this respect.

The Monastic Tradition

One aspect of Augustine's thought that is very fruitful for a reflection on Christian friendship is his theology of the monastic or cenobitic life. For him, the desire for solitude ("flight from the world") or the monastery as a school of Christian perfection takes second place to understanding the monastic community as an expression of brotherly love:

> See, how good and pleasant it is to live as brothers all together! *(Psalm 132:1). These words of the Psalter, this sweet sound, this pleasing melody, in the song as well as in the mind, gave birth to monasteries. By this sound were roused brothers who desired to live in unity; this verse was their trumpet-call. It rang out across the whole world, and those who were divided came together.* (Commentary on Psalm 132, 2)

Augustine was, of course, not the only one to emphasize this dimension of religious life. His slightly older contemporary, Saint Basil of Caesarea, was perhaps the man who, more than anyone else, gave normative shape to monasticism in the Eastern church and also influenced the West through Saint Benedict. Basil's Great Rule for monks contains an entire chapter (Q. 7) demonstrating the superiority of the cenobitic form of religious life to the hermitic, quoting among other texts Matthew 5 ("Let your light shine before others") and Acts 2 and 4 ("The believers lived together … and had one heart and one soul").

Despite these illustrious examples, it would not be completely true to think that, in the history of monasticism or the religious life, friendship has always maintained pride of place. The reason was essentially a practical or pastoral one. Within a community, human friendships, notably among brothers or sisters with little experience of the spiritual life, could easily have a divisive effect on the whole body, leading to the formation of cliques or factions, even if of only two members. Upon reflection, it is clear that the problem is not friendship between Christians as such, but an exclusive outlook that bases friendship on intensity of affection or individual inclinations and that does not allow itself to be transfigured by Christ's love, which is personal and universal at the same time. The solution to the difficulty lies ultimately in fostering growth in the inner life and the capacity for discernment. In practice, however, it often seemed easiest to deal with the matter simply by prohibiting outright "particular attachments" in religious life. In later centuries, this prohibition became a commonplace of formation to community life and to the celibate ministry. In their understandable zeal to avoid the dangers of uncontrolled affectivity, the superiors seemed never to realize that they were courting an even greater danger, that of eliminating the human dimension of Christian love, reducing it to a kind of vague and ultimately abstract goodwill by which all are "loved" in general, and no one in practice. Worse still, in many cases they drove human friendship underground and caused it to be viewed as somehow incompatible with the Gospel or at least worthy of suspicion—an attitude whose nefarious consequences are still with us today.

Aelred

Although the theme of friendship never acquired majority status in Christian spirituality, it nonetheless remained a strong undercurrent that came to the surface at various times and places across the centuries. In the history of monasticism, the clearest example comes to us from the twelfth century, from a monk active during the early years of the Cistercian reform of the Benedictine tradition, linked to the name of Saint Bernard of Clairvaux—Aelred, brother and then abbot of the monastery of Rievaulx in northern England (1110-67), referred to by his contemporaries as the "Bernard of the North." Some twelve centuries after Cicero and seven after Augustine, Aelred achieved the impressive feat of rewriting the Roman philosopher's dialogue on friendship along the lines of the experience of the bishop of Hippo: Augustine's *Confessions* was arguably his favorite book. In Aelred's writings, notably *The Mirror of Charity* and *Spiritual Friendship*, pagan and Christian notions of friendship finally come close to being reconciled in a harmonious whole.

The Mirror of Charity is fundamentally a theological anthropology, in other words an attempt to answer the question "What is a human being?" on the basis of a consideration of human love (*amor*). The work can be best read as a detailed expansion of a single phrase at the beginning of Augustine's *Confessions*: "You have made us for yourself, Lord, and our hearts can never rest until they rest in you" (*Confessions*, I, 1). As one commentator puts it,

> *[Aelred's] approach to the mystery of God begins with the study of created love: considering love in man leads us to contemplate love in God. The soul is the image, the sign and the need of God, above all by its love; if love tends towards God, that is because it is a gift of God and wants to return to its source; the capacity created in it is a call to cling to God, according to the law of the return to God: "like seeks like."* [29]

Communion with God is the goal of all human desiring and striving, our Sabbath rest. And yet Aelred, with a sure instinct for Gospel truth, does not exalt the love we have for God in a way that denigrates love of our fellows:

> *This perspective of God-Charity is the theological summit of Aelred's* Speculum Caritatis, *and yet to remain there would certainly not let us grasp the whole of the Abbot of Rievaulx's thinking concerning the meaning of man and his divine destiny. The human soul is indeed called to resemble God, but a God who is Love and Trinity, and whose life is communion with other persons in the transcendent unity of one and the same nature: "Mutual... affection, ... delicious embrace, this most happy charity by which the Father rests in the Son and the Son in the Father"* (Spec. I, 5).[30]

This vision leads to a consideration of human friendship, seen as a privileged way to make divine love or charity real here on earth. Aelred continued this reflection in a second book, *Spiritual Friendship*, which is nothing other than a transposition of Cicero's *De Amicitia* into a Christian key. Along the lines of Augustine's letter to Marcianus, Aelred explains that Cicero's definition of friendship is fulfilled when friends are made and held on account of Christ: "For what more sublime can be said of friendship, what more true, what more profitable, than that it ought to, and is proved to, begin in Christ, continue in Christ, and be perfected in Christ?"[31]

One of the characteristics of friendship in Greek and Roman antiquity was its aristocratic or elite nature: it was a relationship for the few, an intense sharing of life and thought requiring inclination, ability, and a significant investment of time and energy. And then, with the appearance of Christianity, the notion of a love both universal and concrete came on to the scene. It is interesting to see how Aelred strives to reconcile these two outlooks. In Book I, Ivo, his dialogue partner, raises precisely the objection we have just evoked, stating that if friendship remains so rare even after Christ's coming, it would be a cause of frustration (*Spiritual Friendship*, I, 25). Aelred replies that, in fact, friendship did increase after Christ, for the early Christians, who had one heart and one soul, were ready to give their lives in great numbers for their fellow-believers (*Spiritual Friendship*, I, 27-30). Ivo then wonders whether there is in fact no difference between friendship and Christian love or charity (*Spiritual Friendship*, I, 31), and this leads Aelred to backtrack a bit:

On the contrary; there is a vast difference; for divine authority approves that more are to be received into the bosom of charity than into the embrace of friendship. For we are compelled by the law of charity to receive in the embrace of love not only our friends but also our enemies. But only those do we call friends to whom we can fearlessly entrust our heart and all its secrets; those, too, who, in turn, are bound to us by the same law of faith and security. (*Spiritual Friendship*, I, 32)

On the one hand, there is false friendship, that is, friendship not based on true love, and, on the other, there is love for those whom strictly speaking we cannot call friends. Later on, Aelred explains that before sin entered the world, friendship and charity went hand in hand.

But after the fall of the first man, when with the cooling of charity concupiscence made secret inroads and caused private good to take precedence over the common weal, it corrupted the splendor of friendship and charity through avarice and envy, introducing contentions, emulations, hates and suspicions because the morals of men had been corrupted. From that time the good distinguished between charity and friendship, observing that love ought to be extended even to the hostile and perverse, while no union of will and ideas can exist between the good and wicked. And so friendship which, like charity, was first persevered among all by all, remained according to the natural law among the few good. (*Spiritual Friendship*, I, 58-59)

At the end of time, in the Kingdom, friendship will once again be

universal: "here [it] belongs to the few because few are good, but
there [it] belongs to all where all are good" (*Spiritual Friendship*,
III, 80).[32]

The Abbot of Rievaulx thus offers a nuanced appreciation
of human friendship as finding its fullness in Christ, potentially
open to all but, in fact, limited by the conditions of life here on
earth. Making and keeping true friends is not automatic: it must be
cultivated. This is a process involving four stages: selection, pro-
bation, admission, and, finally, perfect harmony in matters human
and divine with charity and benevolence (*Spiritual Friendship*,
III, 8). Friendship requires loyalty, right intention, discretion and
patience (*Spiritual Friendship*, III, 61-76). It is not just a matter
of feelings (*Spiritual Friendship*, I, 39-41, II, 57), but also of reason and conscious choice (*Spiritual Friendship*, III, 2-3, 54). True
friendship is eternal (*Spiritual Friendship*, I, 21, 23, 68, III, 44, 48).
Coming from God, it is also a stage in the love and knowledge of
God (*Spiritual Friendship*, II, 14-18); it opens human beings to the
mystery of Christ:

> *Not too steep or unnatural does the ascent appear from Christ, as
> the inspiration of the love by which we love our friend, to Christ
> giving himself to us as our Friend for us to love, so that charm
> may follow upon charm, sweetness upon sweetness and affection
> upon affection. And thus, friend cleaving to friend in the spirit
> of Christ, is made with Christ but one heart and one soul, and so
> mounting aloft through degrees of love to friendship with Christ.*
> (*Spiritual Friendship*, II, 20-21)

Clearly, for Aelred, there is nothing more sacred or profitable on earth than true friendship in Christ (*Spiritual Friendship*, II, 9). This is why he can even ask, putting it into the mouth of one of his conversational partners, whether "God is friendship." And he replies, adapting the words of Saint John: "He that abides in friendship, abides in God, and God in him" (*Spiritual Friendship*, I, 70).

Aquinas

What was only implicit in Aelred's writings, namely, the identification of Christian love, *agapē* or *caritas*, with friendship, becomes explicit in the thought of the man many view—inaccurately—as a dry scholastic theologian lost in his books, the Dominican scholar Thomas Aquinas (1225-74). According to Carmichael,

> *Thomas was the only scholastic to define Christian love,* caritas, *fully and in every respect as friendship,* amicitia. *He developed this teaching steadily and consistently throughout his career, from his early commentary on the* Sentences *to his final* Summa Theologica.[33]

Taking his cues more from the Gospel and from Aristotle than from Cicero, Aquinas is not concerned primarily with relationships among human beings, but rather with that between human beings and God, which makes all the more surprising his insistence on friendship. What undoubtedly oriented him in this direction, in addition to John 15:15, was Aristotle's understanding of friendship as based on *koinōnia*, things held in common. Friendship is the highest form of love because, unlike *eros*, the love of desire, it is by definition mutual; it is an expression of communion. Friendship

requires a kind of mutual loving, because a friend is a friend to his friend. Such a mutual goodwill is founded upon a kind of communication. Since there is a communication between man and God, inasmuch as he communicates his happiness to us, some kind of friendship must needs be based on this same communication, of which it is written (1 Cor 1:9): God is faithful: by whom you are called into the fellowship *(societas, koinonia)* of his Son. *The love which is based on this communication is charity: wherefore it is evident that charity is the friendship of man for God.*[34]

But how is such reciprocity possible between two such different partners—the Creator and the creature, the Source of all life and beings who exist in a state of total dependence? Thomas finds an answer in the utterly free and generous act of a God who communicates his own life—his happiness, he says in the above quote—to human beings, going down to our level to bring us up to the level of the divine. And so, through Christ, we become friends of God.

The love God bestows on us overflows to inform our relationship with others. Following Augustine, Thomas enumerates four objects of *caritas*: God, one's neighbor, one's body, and oneself (*Summa Theologica*, II-II, 25.12). If *caritas* is essentially friendship, then it follows that we are called to friendship with all people for the sake of Christ. Here, the difference in outlook between Aelred and Aquinas is most salient. Aelred, like Augustine, starts from concrete experiences of human friendship, understood with the aid of Cicero, and then reflects on how faith in Christ transforms and extends these relationships. Thomas begins with a more theological and philosophical conception of friendship-love and uses it to explain *caritas*, God's love in us shown first of all in our communion with God and secondarily in our relationships in the created order. He is thus not primarily concerned with how far friendships can be extended; what he needs to explain is how we can call friendship that love which Christ invites us to extend even to our enemies. His answer is that "since by charity we love our neighbor because of God, the more someone loves God the more they show love for their neighbor, without taking their enmity into account. It is as if someone who has a great love for another person loves their children because of that love, even if they are his enemies" (*Summa Theologica*, II-II, 25.8). Christians love others as beings created by God and called by God to share his own life; they are thus loved at least as potential friends of God and therefore of believers.

Aquinas's seemingly more abstract notion of friendship provides a necessary corrective to Augustine and Aelred. Their problem, never entirely resolved, was how to reconcile friendship of the few with the Gospel's call to universality. Thomas reminds us that, in the final analysis, we love others because of God's love revealed and communicated to us in Christ, and this love is, by its very nature, all inclusive. The challenge here is to keep this love from becoming a merely abstract category and to discover how to enflesh it, so to speak, in different kinds of specific relationships.

Modern Times

Let us close this brief survey of friendship across the ages by selecting, almost by chance, a few significant figures out of a host of others. We can begin with Jeremy Taylor (1613-1667), an Anglican clergyman who wrote, in response to a question by the writer Katherine Philips, a *Discourse of the Nature and Offices of Friendship* (1657). Taylor integrates well the thinking of the writers we have already investigated. The Gospel made friendship universal:

> *Christian charity is friendship to all the world; and when friendships were the noblest things in the world, charity was little, like the sun drawn in at a chink, or his beams drawn into the centre of a burning-glass; but Christian charity is friendship, expanded like the face of the sun when it mounts above the eastern hills. . . . And the more we love, the better we are, and the greater our friendships are, the dearer we are to God; let them be as dear, and let them be as perfect, and let them be as many as you can; there is no danger in it; only when the restraint begins, there begins our imperfection.*[35]

Still, for Taylor the universal reach of friendship does not exclude particular affinity between certain people, "even as our blessed Saviour himself loved S. John and Lazarus by a special love, which was signified by special treatments."[36]

Two centuries later, another Anglican clergyman, preaching on the feast of Saint John the Evangelist, likewise pointed out the "remarkable circumstance" that the Son of God had a private friend. John Henry Newman (1801-90) uses this to explain that Christian love is not abstract or general but concrete and particular, beginning with those closest to us in order to go out to all: "the best preparation for loving the world at large, and loving it duly and wisely, is to cultivate an intimate friendship and affection towards those who are immediately about us."[37] A few years later, it was not by chance that the last sermon he preached in the Church of England was entitled "The Parting of Friends."

Despite enormous differences of time, place, and perhaps temperament, in the topic that interests us there are astonishing parallels between Newman and Saint Augustine. For both of them, friendship was one of the mainstays of existence. Newman kept up an extensive correspondence his whole life long with scores of friends, both male and female. The extent of his friendships did not militate against their depth: he always cultivated particular relationships of great intensity. Forsaking his career at Oxford in 1842 and settling in the village of Littlemore, he surrounded himself with a group of like-minded friends striving to progress in holiness together, awakening suspicions that he was creating an Anglo-Catholic monastery. After becoming a Roman Catholic, he founded in England the Congregation of the Oratory, attracted by St. Philip Neri's vision of a flexible community of priests living together in mutual affection, without taking vows, and undertaking different ministries. Again like Augustine, Newman never attempted to develop a theology or ecclesiology based on friendship; for him it was more a matter of practice than theory.

The German pastor and theologian Dietrich Bonhoeffer (1906-45), active in the Resistance against Hitler, has already been mentioned in these pages. In him we encounter once again a profile that has already become familiar to us. A man, on the one hand, capable of deep friendships and, on the other, profoundly

convinced that the renewal of the church depended on the rediscovery of community life, he seems never to have made any explicit link between the two. And this, despite the fact that he made
the acquaintance of the man who was to become his closest friend
and disciple, Eberhard Bethge, at the "underground seminary" he
set up for the Confessing Church in Finkenwalde. In Bonhoeffer's
mind, Finkenwalde was not only to be a place of study but was
also meant to offer an experience of community life, animated by
a core group having a distinctively cenobitic flavor. Unfortunately, the experience was cut short by government opposition and,
later on, by Bonhoeffer's imprisonment and execution.

It was seemingly only at the end of his life, in one of his letters
to Bethge from prison (January 23, 1944), that Bonhoeffer com-
mented explicitly on friendship and then only in response to his
friend's reflections. Along with a poem written later that year for
Bethge, entitled "The Friend," these are the only lines we have
from him on the subject. It is clear, nonetheless, that he considers friendship one of life's highest goods and emphasizes strongly
its rootedness in the domain of freedom: by its very nature it has
no ulterior motives. In a world dominated more and more by efficiency, reinforced by the culturally Prussian-Protestant accent on
duty, Bonhoeffer estimates that henceforth only the church can and
should defend the realm of freedom and therefore of friendship.
At the same time, he views friendship as fundamentally different
from brotherhood in Christ. Here, he is clearly under the sway of
a Lutheran—and ultimately Augustinian—tendency to separate,
and even to oppose, nature and grace. This stands out in the first
chapter of *Life Together*, his small and influential book inspired by
the Finkenwalde experiment. It is marked by a strong mistrust for

anything that exalts human choices and feelings in Christian community, rooted in a sharp distinction between the "spiritual" and the "psychological," between *agapē* and *eros*. Friendship apparently belongs to the latter domain, and thus is, at best, a "penultimate" reality, to use a category from his later unfinished work, *Ethics*.

Bonhoeffer's life was tragically cut short by his untimely death at the age of 39, so we must be wary in judging his thought, which remained in process. He had an uncommon capacity for spiritual and intellectual growth, and it is not impossible that, had he lived, he would have come to a vision of the church, *sanctorum communio*, as a community of friends.

We turn next to Bonhoeffer's contemporary Simone Weil (1909-43), an intellectual also active in the Resistance, but in France. Born in a nonpracticing Jewish family, she was deeply influenced by the Gospel, although she made a well-thought-out personal decision not to seek baptism. In her book *Waiting on God*, she analyzes friendship from a completely different starting point than the other thinkers we have examined, though there is an unexpected parallel with Bonhoeffer in her insistence on freedom. Natural affection tends to be based on a relationship of necessity, and necessity in the long run engenders hatred and disgust. Pure friendship thus surpasses nature: it is a miracle by which necessity and respect for the other's autonomy and freedom are reconciled. It maintains a distance that gives it an "objective" quality, insofar as it affirms the other as other. In this sense it is universal. "It consists in loving a human being as we should like to be able to love each soul in particular and all those who go to make up the human race." Moreover, friendship in obedience to Christ has a sacramental character: "'Where there are two or three gathered together in my name there I am in the midst of them.' Pure friendship is an image of the original and perfect friendship that belongs to the Trinity and is the very essence of God. It is impossible for two human beings to be one while scrupulously respecting the distance that separates them, unless God is present in each of them."[38]

These pages have limited themselves almost exclusively to Christian witnesses from the West, so it is fitting to mention here a representative of the Eastern Church, who was also a twentieth-century martyr, not of Hitler but of Stalin. Pavel Florensky (1882-1937) was a Russian scientist, inventor, philosopher, and priest, who was eventually condemned to exile and prison camp before being executed by the Soviet secret police. His multifaceted genius and encyclopedic range of interests have led some to call him the Russian Leonardo da Vinci. Florensky's principal published work, *The Pillar and Ground of the Truth: An Essay in Orthodox Theodicy in Twelve Letters*, contains a long treatise on friendship (Letter XI), beginning with a masterful analysis of the "four loves" in the Greek world, both classical and Christian, that predates C. S. Lewis by several decades. It also includes a series of texts from the Greek Church Fathers on the importance of friendship. According to Florensky, pagan society was founded on *eros* as a personal principle and *storḡe* as a generic one. In Christian society, on the other hand, these have been replaced, respectively, by a spiritualized and transformed *philia* and *agapē*. The latter was embodied in the common life of the early Christians, and later on in parishes and cenobitic communities, and is symbolized by the term "brother." Friendship, on the other hand, refers to deeper and more intimate relationships that can go to the point of "mystical oneness," and is shown emblematically in the New Testament by the sending out of the disciples in pairs. "The agapic and philic aspects of church life, brotherhood and friendship, run parallel to each other in many ways. (. . .) At points of their highest significance, at their peaks, the two currents (. . .) strive to merge fully. (. . .) Nevertheless, these two currents are irreducible to each other. Each is necessary in its own way in the church economy, just as and in connection with which personal creativity and the continuity of tradition are both necessary, each in its own way."[39]

Our final example comes from the writings of two twentieth-century German Lutheran theologians, Jürgen Moltmann and Elisabeth Moltmann-Wendel. The former, in his book *The Church in the Power of the Spirit* (1975), adds to the traditional titles of the Savior "Jesus the Friend," claiming that it describes best "the inner relationship both of the communion with God and of the human community."[40] "Friend" is not a title but a personal qualification; when all social roles have been left behind, friendship remains. It is the positive side of a classless society with no relationships of domination. Friendship between human beings and God is shown, above all, in confident prayer and divine listening (cf. Luke 11:5ff). It is characterized by freedom and joy. Modern society has privatized friendship, turning it into a predominantly emotional and individual reality. Christians must therefore "de-privatize" friendship, rediscovering its public character. The task of the church is to live out this friendship: "The *congregatio sanctorum*, the community of brethren, is really the fellowship of friends who live in the friendship of Jesus and spread friendship in society, by going to encounter the forsaken with affection and the despised with respect."[41] The necessary reform of the church involves essentially a rebirth of community, of friendship, at a grassroots level. Without this, any institutional reforms will remain a dead letter.

In her book *Rediscovering Friendship* (2000), Elisabeth Molt-mann-Wendel examines the experience of women to propose a reflection on the figure of Mary Magdalene and her relationship to Jesus as a way of deepening the notion of a church built on friendship. She looks at tenderness and *eros* as "the stormy first steps on the way to a culture of friendship," a friendship that reaches out to include one's own body and indeed the earth itself.[42]

TOWARD A THEOLOGY OF FRIENDSHIP

The notion of friendship used to describe Christ's message and the life of his followers thus has a very long history. While almost never occupying center stage, it constantly reappears down through the ages. To close this chapter, I will attempt to gather together some of the strands of this history into a more unified outlook.

The historical survey in the preceding pages shows that an investigation of this topic by nonbelievers can be based either on concrete experiences of human friendship (Cicero) or on more abstract philosophical reflection (Empedocles, Aristotle). Christians reflecting on friendship can, in their turn, begin either with the human side of things, as did Augustine and Aelred, or else from the side of God, by reflecting on the Gospel. Saint Thomas Aquinas, although he relies heavily on Aristotle's analysis of friendship, in fact chooses the second course. The key counter-argument he brings forward against the objections to the question "Is *caritas* friendship?" (*Summa Theologica*, II-II, 23.1) comes not from Aristotle but from the Fourth Gospel. If we wish to reason theologically, we should follow Thomas's lead and begin with divine Revelation.

In Matthew 11:19, Jesus is called "a friend of tax-collectors and sinners." Although this is intended as an insult, it indicates well Jesus' way of acting, shown, for example, in the scene where he shares table fellowship with these same outcasts, something quite shocking for the pious believers of his day (Matthew 9:10ff). Jesus then describes himself as a physician whose priority is to take care of those who are ill. In him, God is revealed as the One who goes first of all toward the people who are furthest away, to bring them into fellowship with himself and consequently with one another. If, following Matthew 11:19, we characterize this attitude as friendship, we can say that divine love becomes real essentially in the endeavor to *make friends*, doing everything possible to transform those previously ill disposed or indifferent into people with whom a sharing of life is possible.

Although he does not use the words "friend" or "friendship," Saint Paul likewise considers the transition from the state of being "outside the circle" to being within as characteristic of God's activity in Christ. Paul calls this movement from exclusion to inclusion "reconciliation":

> *God demonstrates his own love for us insofar as Christ died for us while we were still sinners. (...) If, while we were enemies, we were reconciled to God by the death of his Son, how much more, once reconciled, will we be saved by his life. Not only that, but we can trust confidently in God through our Lord, Jesus Christ, through whom at present we have obtained reconciliation.* (Romans 5:8, 10-11; cf. 2 Corinthians 5:17-21)

God's primary intention was to reconcile the universe to himself in Christ, and this movement from enmity to friendship occurs definitively in Christ's self-giving on the cross (Colossians 1:19-

22). At the same time, the texts just quoted from Matthew's Gospel show that Jesus' activity on earth already reveals the face of a God passionately concerned with turning enemies into friends.

If the image of the outcasts of society gathered at table with Jesus strikingly expresses the reason for his existence, concretely it is the community of his disciples that shares Jesus' table over the long haul. It is therefore not surprising that, in John's Gospel, Jesus refers to them as his friends:

> *I do not call you servants any longer, because a servant does not know what his master is doing. Instead I call you friends, because I have made known to you everything I have heard from my Father. You were not the ones who chose me; rather I chose you and appointed you to go and bear fruit, and your fruit will last, so that whatever you ask the Father in my name he will give to you. This is my command: that you love one another.* (John 15:15-17)

We have repeatedly seen that friendship-love is characterized by a third element that the friends have in common; this love is essentially triadic. In this Gospel passage, Jesus explains that the disciples are now his friends because he has chosen them and handed on to them the entire message the Father gave him. The common element that creates friendship between Jesus and his followers is thus the revelation that comes in the final analysis from the unseen God, in other words the answer to the questions "Who is God?" and "Who are we?" Elsewhere, John calls this "the truth" (see John 8:32, 14:6, 17:17, 18:37). This truth is not just intellectual; it involves a way of life, summed up in the command to love one another. Moreover, we should not imagine this commandment as simply an outward law; it is the gift of God's own love; it is God's own life at work in us. Extrapolating a bit, we can therefore say that the common element, in Aristotle's language the *koinōnia*, which makes us friends of Jesus, is, first of all, his message, the Gospel, but even more deeply the life of love that he shares with the Father and transmits to us. In a word, it is "the Spirit of truth" (John 14:17), which gives life (John 6:63) and which leads Jesus' followers into the fullness of the truth (John 14:26, 16:13).

If what makes one a Christian, then, is sharing in the love that the Father communicates to the Son and the Son communicates to us, it follows that to live out our identity, we must practice this same love. In short, we are called to *make friends* and to *be friends*. These parallel notions can help us bridge two dichotomies that have sometimes raised problems in trying to understand God's universal love, on the one hand, and friendship, on the other. First of all, people sometimes wonder why, whereas Matthew and Luke speak of the love of enemies (see Matthew 5:43ff; Luke 6:27ff), the Johannine writings mention almost exclusively believers loving "one another." John is certainly not trying to deny the universal character of Christian love; rather, his words point to the fullest realization of this love, a love that is "brought to perfection" (1 John 4:12; cf. 1 John 4:17-18, 2:5) in mutuality. Love of enemies corresponds rather to the attempt to *make friends*. When these former enemies or strangers have been brought into the circle of friendship by opening their hearts to the love shown to them and responding with love in return, the friendship-love, which is *caritas* in its essence, is present and can start to grow.

On another level, we have seen that the classical notion of friendship emphasizes so strongly the quality of the sharing between friends that it tends to restrict friendship to a few intense relationships. Christian authors have attempted, with more or less success, to reconcile this restricted understanding of friendship with the universal outlook of their faith. Perhaps the above categories can help us find a solution. The Gospel's call to make friends is universal, insofar as all human beings are approached as potential friends. When someone responds to this offer, the mutual love of friendship becomes active in the relationship. But here too, the friendship must be developed, and this will be determined in part by the human qualities and possibilities of the individuals involved. Being friends is not an all-or-nothing situation, nor is it a static state of affairs. Friendship must be cultivated: it exists on a dynamic continuum running from a simple sharing in common activities and a common outlook to a lifelong companionship where the friend is truly an *alter ego*, another self. To grow in friendship, ultimately it is one's own heart that must be transformed; it must become deeper and more encompassing. The limit case is the heart of Christ himself. To the extent that someone approaches this, they become able to be a friend to all. We can fittingly close this chapter with a quotation from Charles de Foucauld (1858-1916), hermit in the Sahara and apostle to the Touaregs, whose life inspired several spiritual families in the church:

> *Every Christian must see each human being as a beloved brother or sister. A sinner, an enemy of God, the Christian must see as someone ill, very ill, and should feel a deep pity and should care for that person as for a wayward brother or sister. Non-Christians may have a Christian for their enemy; the Christian must always be a loving friend towards every person and have towards them all the same feelings as Jesus had in his Heart.*[43]

4

A Parable of Community

An abstract friendship is a contradiction in terms. As already stated in the introduction to this book, the initial impulse for writing it was an autobiographical one. It arose out of my experience in the community to which I belong, particularly in its relationship to the young visitors who for years now have taken up a good deal of our time and energy. This context allows us, before drawing some general conclusions regarding the importance of friendship in understanding the Christian message and the life of the church, to examine more closely a concrete illustration of this. Such an illustration should help us grasp better what being friends in Christ is and what it is not. If this chapter, then, speaks exclusively of the Taizé Community and its ministry, it goes without saying that this is not because it is the only possible example or even necessarily the best one. It is simply the one I know best and the one that has led me to reflect on this topic. In describing how we live, my intention is, above all, to flesh out the notion of universal friendship presented in these pages, which otherwise could seem theoretical or even utopian.

BROTHERS ON ACCOUNT OF CHRIST AND THE GOSPEL

Many people know Taizé primarily through the repetitive chants used in many churches around the world or else as a style of meditative prayer rooted in singing and silence. For others, especially in Europe, the name evokes a place in eastern France to which young adults flock in large numbers to meet others and to deepen their Christian faith. While all these elements are pieces of the puzzle, what is still lacking is the center that unifies them. At the heart of life on the hill of Taizé, and the source of the worship and music now known on every continent, is a monastic community of over one hundred brothers from twenty-five different countries and from different Christian traditions.

The story of the Taizé Community began at the beginning of the Second World War. In August 1940, a twenty-five-year-old theology student from French-speaking Switzerland, Roger Schütz-Marsauche, left his home and crossed the border into France. Concerned about the growing individualism in society that was leaving its mark on the church as well and convinced that, in addition to words, there was a need for existential signs to manifest the truth and beauty of the Gospel, he was led to examine the age-old tradition of intentional community life in the church and its possible relevance for our time.

The young man who was to become Brother Roger was not interested in creating a community merely, or even primarily, for the sake of those who would become its members. It is striking to realize how, from the very beginning, he justified cenobitic life on the basis of its sign value. In a small book he published in 1944, when the nascent community numbered only four members, he wrote,

> *The preaching of the Word must always be completed by that of example. Thus, a resident community could be, in the Church, an image of the Christian community, an image that is alive, with clear contours, and in this way more accessible to the individualistic outlook of our century.*[44]

In those first years, he often repeated the words of Jesus in John's Gospel (17:21-23): one, so that the world may believe. And in another early work he explained,

> *our sole desire was to be a family of brothers committed to following Christ, as an existential sign of the communion of the People of God. Life in community is a living microcosm of the Church, an image on a small scale containing the whole reality of the People of God. And so the humble sign of a community can find a resonance far beyond the limitations of the individuals who make it up. The world of today needs images more than ideas. No idea can be accepted unless it is clothed in visible reality, otherwise it is only ideology. However weak the sign, it takes on its full value when it is a living reality.* (DP 59; cf. UP 19-20)[45]

Many years later, his focus remained the same:

> *What are you, little community? (...) Perhaps a group of men united to be stronger, humanly speaking, in order to realize their*

own aims? Not that either. So could we be living a common life in order to be comfortable together? No, the community would then become an end in itself, and that would allow us to settle down in cozy little nests. Being happy together? Certainly, but in the context of the offering of our lives. What are you, little community, spread out in different parts of the world? A parable of communion, a simple reflection of that unique communion which is the Body of Christ, his Church, and therefore a ferment in the human family. (HT 52)

Image, sign, microcosm, reflection—in the *Rule of Taizé*, the text Brother Roger composed in 1951-52 and rewrote constantly throughout his life, in order to set down some essential elements of the adventure upon which he had embarked with his brothers, we find a key expression that in some sense recapitulates his vision of the importance of Christian community:

The Lord Christ, in his compassion and his love for you, has chosen you to be in the Church a sign of brotherly love. It is his will that with your brothers you live the parable of community. (PC 43)

A community as a parable, a parable of unity, or of communion. The word "parable," in addition to expressing the fact that the community exists to communicate the Gospel message and not for itself, emphasizes that the specific details of the life are not important in themselves; it does not intend to offer itself as a model or an example to be imitated. Taizé is one particular way of living out the "brotherly love" that all Christians are called to put into practice. Just as Jesus told many different stories to illustrate his teaching, there can and should be a host of different lived-out parables, perhaps as many as there are believers.

One of the parables of Jesus that was always particularly relevant to Brother Roger in explaining the importance of community life was that of the leaven in the dough (Matthew 13:33):

> *Today as never before, if it is filled with the sap proper to it, if it overflows with the freshness of brotherly life that is its reason for being, community life is a leaven in the dough. It contains within itself a potentially explosive force. It can raise mountains of indifference and bring to people an irreplaceable quality of Christ's presence. In the darkest periods, very often a small number of women and men, spread across the world, were able to reverse the course of historical evolutions, because they hoped against all hope. What seemed doomed to disintegration entered instead into the current of a new dynamism.* (UP 13-14)

Brother Roger's vision of community life thus unites, in ways reminiscent of the Johannine writings in the New Testament, mutual love among believers in Christ and a universal outlook. The two realities are not in tension, as if one had to choose which to give priority to, nor are they simply two separate dimensions of a life of discipleship. Communion among believers is primordial, since it expresses the basic meaning of their Christian identity (cf. John 13:34-35). This communion is shown most visibly, as we see in the Acts of the Apostles, by spiritual and material sharing among the disciples of Christ, who consider themselves members of one and the same family—in short by life in community. And this life should be, as far as possible, a parable that "speaks for itself" without explanations (DF 32); it is, beyond any verbal preaching, the most effective proclamation of the Christian message. A Christian community thus exists not for itself, but for the church and for all humanity. Or, more exactly, its deepest rationale is to give expression to human relationships of goodwill and kindness, which are rooted in a relationship with God through Christ, and which contain a dynamism that inexorably extends outward to "the whole world" (cf. 1 John 2:2).

FRIENDSHIP, THE FACE OF CHRIST

The founder of Taizé did not hesitate, when necessary, to use the word "friendship" in the context of this vocation to live for Christ. For him, friendship was in some sense the human side of the church:

> *Faith is not born of human friendship, but it does find support there. Through a series of friendships, going all the way back to the first community of Christians, so that what counts is not my faith, but the faith of the Church.* (VP 73)

At the same time, a passionate concern for reconciliation among Christians led Brother Roger to make friends with a great many different kinds of people across the world (DP 33; UP 38). He particularly valued friendship with nonbelievers (VP 75). And some of his friendships, even of short duration, were of "rare intimacy," so that he could write about them: "There is no more luminous reflection of God's face on this earth" (VP 73-

74) and "Friendship is the face of Christ" (F 73).

For all that, Brother Roger's celebration of friendship was not uncritical. First of all, in order to be authentic, all human intimacy must become aware of and consent to its limits:

> *Any self-examination leads to the conclusion that every intimate relationship, even between the most united partners, inevitably has its limitations. Beyond them, we are alone. Anyone who refuses to accept this natural order of things will, as a result of his refusal, find himself in revolt. Accepting our fundamental aloneness sets us on the road to peace, and allows the Christian to discover a previously unknown dimension of his relationship with God. Acceptance of this portion of loneliness, a condition of every human life, fosters intimacy with the One who rescues us from the overwhelming solitude of the man alone with himself.* (DP 75; cf. UP 101-2)

And some years later he asked,

> *Does not the burning thirst for relationships between human beings have its source in the presentiment of another and more essential communion, our relationship with Christ?* (VP 74)

In fact, "our relationship with [Christ] is one of friendship," with periods of seeming indifference followed by new beginnings (WL 52). Since this friendship is rooted and deepened, above all, in a life of prayer, it follows that praying together with others is the most unambiguous image of communion: "it overflows into a celebration of friendship" (F 27). Brother Roger saw clearly that, for a Christian, in the final analysis human friendships were founded in friendship with Christ, in an inner life from which we constantly draw the "living water" of God's love. Where this rootedness is not present, friendship runs the risk of degenerating into a superficial *camaraderie*, an overfamiliarity in danger of masking or even replacing the search for a true communion of hearts and minds. On several occasions, Brother Roger would speak to the brothers about the perils of this *camaraderie*, a French word difficult to translate but that indicates a superficiality in human relations that is, in fact, a caricature of authentic relationships:

> *Those who come to us ... are looking for men who radiate God. This requires a life hidden in God, so that the presence of Christ may be reawakened in us. Preserving a deep inner life, avoiding febrile dispersion, we must look for ways of being at all times men of hospitality and of openness. The overfamiliarity desired by certain visitors would quickly give the lie to our vocation and disappoint the expectations of the visitors themselves. Beneficial neither to us nor to them, the spirit of* camaraderie *casts a pall over our vocation and discredits it. It keeps alive an illusion of communication.* (UP 38-39)

Similarly, the *Rule of Taizé* encourages us never to lose sight of the fact that true friendship is extremely demanding: "There is no friendship without purifying suffering. There is no love for our neighbor without the Cross. Only by the Cross can we know the unfathomable depths of love" (PC 32).

TAIZÉ AND THE YOUNG

Beginning gradually through the 1960s, and expanding exponentially in the early 1970s, students and other young adults began making their way to the hill of Taizé. The brothers had organized some modest work camps and other gatherings, especially for the young, and all of a sudden, essentially by word of mouth, their numbers started to mushroom. It should be remembered that these were years of dramatic changes in society, when the "baby-boomers" of the postwar period were reaching maturity and searching for new answers for their personal life and for society, as well as for the church. Even if the brothers were at first caught unawares by this unforeseen development, there could be no doubt that Taizé would rise to the challenge, given the community's basic reason for being. Brother Roger scarcely hesitated: it was essential to welcome the young searchers, to listen to their questions, frustrations, and demands, and to share with them what was most important in the community's own life and faith. This willingness to offer hospitality would require significant changes in the community's way of life: the clearest sign of this was the decision, for Easter 1972, to tear down the rear wall of the recently constructed Church of Reconciliation and attach a large tent in order to accommodate the unexpectedly huge crowds of pilgrims.

So Taizé became a place where young people come to congregate. Forty years later, the coming and going of young visitors shows little or no signs of abating. This is probably just as significant as the fact that they came in the first place. The youth of 2010 are not those of 1970, nor indeed those of 1990. And yet they keep coming.

Why do they come? That is the magic question we are constantly asked, and our first reply is to say that we remain just as astonished as anyone else. The brothers had no particular training or preparation for youth ministry. They simply tried to respond to the challenge as best they could, in a way consonant with their own life and faith. This is certainly one of the reasons that a stay in Taizé is seen as meaningful by the young people who come. They have never had the impression that they were the "targets" of a conscious and intentional strategy. Instead, they were invited to take part in a joint undertaking that had meaning, first of all, for the brothers themselves, eventually referred to as a "pilgrimage of trust on earth."

If you ask the young adults themselves why they come to Taizé, you will receive a whole range of answers. On one end of the continuum, you find people active in a Christian congregation or movement who come intentionally in order to deepen their faith. At the other extreme, there are those who know very little about Christianity and come because they are intrigued, usually after hearing of the experience from their peers. In general, young adults arrive in Taizé for the first time out of curiosity or, more precisely, through a kind of "contagion" from other young people. Those who make their way to the hill of Taizé are so diverse in their expectations and motivations that it is probably futile to look for a unity of purpose. It is more meaningful to ask what they find there that leads them to want to share the experience with others and to come back themselves.

When you ask a group of young pilgrims what has struck them most during a week spent in Taizé, you inevitably hear variations of three answers, always the same. They mention the chance to meet others of the same age from a great diversity of backgrounds, the experience of community prayer, and the simplicity of life on the hill. Let us look at each of these three facets of life in Taizé in turn, to discover what light they shed on our reflections.

LIFE IN A GLOBAL VILLAGE

When young adults come to Taizé for the first time, most typically on a Sunday afternoon in the summer, they encounter a buzzing confusion of languages, faces, and styles—three or four thousand people their own age, from over fifty different countries, from many Christian denominations, movements, and backgrounds. No wonder, then, that for some the first impression is so unsettling that they are ready to turn round and go home—as they tell us later on! Soon, however, the bells begin to ring for evening prayer, and the disorganized crowd morphs into a peaceful assembly all facing in the same direction, singing, listening, and sitting in silence. This transition is already a kind of parable of the entire week: aimless diversity turned into harmony by being focused on the one reality able to unite us all without constraint or violence.

During the meetings, visitors to Taizé live side by side with others of the most varied origins. They worship together; listen to reflections on the Bible; discuss in small groups; work, eat, and have fun together; and even sleep in the same cabins and tents. For many, it is the first time they have come to know personally and intimately their peers from other countries and confessions. Prejudices quickly vanish, since they are understandably more difficult to cling to when people are together at close range with the others and can discover, beyond superficial differences, a surprising similarity.

Over the course of the week, bonds inevitably form between the visitors. It is, in fact, striking to see how quickly the population of the hill changes its character from a formless mass to a structured community. As could be expected, the relationships that come into being may be based at first on a surface affinity, on the discovery of mutual interests that may have nothing to do with faith or spirituality. But the quality of life on the hill tends to deepen the bonds that form. Every day, participants listen to a brother speak about a Bible text and try to make it more accessible to them. Following this short talk, they break into small groups and discuss what possible light the text can shed on their own life. Sharing questions about the meaning of life and faith with others from a great variety of backgrounds and experiences, discovering that beyond the differences there are most often common aspirations and common frustrations, is an experience that never fails to have a deep impact on people. It gives concrete and specific content to expressions like "the global village" or "one human family." Born in a society where worldwide communication is taken for granted, young people today have an innate sense of the universal. Through discussing, working, and praying together with people of the same age from across the world, they discover the human face of this universal outlook. It no longer remains abstract or virtual, but rather becomes a flesh-and-blood reality.

Participants in the international meetings in Taizé thus experience Christian communion in a particularly concentrated form. They realize that this communion is both universal and concrete, since it is made up of people from many different countries and backgrounds with specific names and faces. It incorporates their human interests and concerns while going beyond them, since in the final analysis it is rooted in a common experience of searching for the face of God, revealed through Christian prayer and reflection on the Scriptures. That is why, although people are in one another's company only for a few days, the friendships formed tend to last far beyond the time actually spent together. And even when contacts are not kept up over subsequent months and years, the awareness of a common bond does not die: it is not rare for people who have spent time together in Taizé, and happen to meet again a decade or so later, to enter immediately into the same relationship, as if the intervening time did not matter. And, in general, they do not simply speak with nostalgia about the past but continue sharing their personal journeys. It is as if the sharing of such deep realities creates a common belonging that annuls the corrosive effects of time. Friendships formed in Taizé are different, many people say; they do not wear out.

By helping us understand better the character of friendship, this observation can show us a way out of a serious difficulty that besets human relationships today. One of the essential qualities of any authentic friendship is loyalty or faithfulness; without this continuity over time, whereby I trust that the other will be there for me tomorrow just as he or she was yesterday and is today, in fact no relationship exists. And yet it is obvious that contemporary society, focused as it is on immediate gratification, makes any kind of continuity over time extremely problematic. The experience we have just mentioned shows that faithfulness is not rooted in an effort of the will; it is not achieved by moralistic injunctions to remain together. What, then, is the glue that keeps a friendship from dissolving? We have seen over and over again that friendship is triadic in nature; it is based on something held in common. The experience of many people in Taizé testifies to the fact that when this common element goes deep enough, when what is shared touches the very depths of the being, bonds are created that can resist the wear and tear of time. In short, the solidity of a relationship is determined by the *quality* of the sharing in the present; what matters is the level at which the encounter between people takes place. And this leads us naturally to the second important dimension of life in Taizé, its rootedness in a quest for God.

To the Sources of Faith

Taizé invites young and not-so-young individuals to be part of an international and interdenominational community. Now in today's world, where encounters across all kinds of borders are increasingly a rule of life, it is less and less rare to come into contact with others who are different. Surprising affinities can then be discovered, with prejudices giving way to the awareness of all that is held in common. Sometimes, even, such contacts between different people lead to the formation of an association with a shared purpose or goal. And yet all of this, valuable though it may be, does not capture the essence of what happens on the hill in Burgundy.

Taizé is first and foremost a community rooted in a quest for the ground of being we call God, by following the steps of Jesus Christ. Three times a day, the bells start ringing and everything stops. Everybody—permanent residents and visitors—heads for the Church of Reconciliation for a time of common prayer lasting from thirty to forty-five minutes. In the evening, the worship is prolonged by meditative singing, which can go on, for those who wish, until the early hours of the morning. Worship in Taizé is based on the age-old monastic tradition. The services are classical in form, made up of psalms; Scripture readings; intercessions; and, at the center, a long period of silence. When the numbers of visitors began to grow, the community sought ways of making the prayer more accessible to them, while maintaining the sung, biblical, and meditative quality that has always characterized it. That led, among other things, to the creation of the short refrains sung over and over again, first in Latin and then gradually in other languages as well, now associated throughout the world with the name of Taizé. Although the original motivation for this was a practical one, the community soon came to see that, as in many religious traditions, the repetition helped people to go beyond superficial rationality and come closer to the core of their being.

At the heart of every service in Taizé there are eight or more minutes of sitting in silence—a time to rest in God, to let the words listened to and sung penetrate one's being, a way of keeping worship from becoming routine. In the summer months, when five thousand pilgrims, mostly young, are crowded in the church, you can still hear a pin drop during this period of silence. In a world where noise in all its forms tends more and more to pollute the environment, the simple experience of an intentional silence never fails to affect people deeply.

Although the brothers have gone out of their way to make their worship accessible to others, it nonetheless remains the prayer of a monastic community. The young visitors sense that it is not crafted especially for them, and this gives it a certain authenticity in their eyes. In fact, while the style of worship may exercise an immediate fascination, it usually takes a little time for them to feel fully at home there. Is this not because a meditative prayer calls out to a deeper level of their being than the one in which they are accustomed to dwelling? They are challenged to discover a part of themselves often overshadowed by the busyness and the bedlam of contemporary society. Slowly they are awakened to a sense of mystery, to a discovery of the unfathomable depths of existence.

This sense of mystery is fostered by careful attention to the style and atmosphere of the prayer. The Taizé Community has always believed that worship is not just a cerebral process but involves the whole being. As during most of the Christian centuries, and still today in the Eastern church, liturgy should help all the aspects of a person enter into a relationship with the Source of life. In our community, using very simple means (candles, icons, soft lighting, some bricks and some cloth, etc.), we attempt to create a space that facilitates openness and inner quiet. It would be true to say that a focus on beauty and simplicity are the hallmarks of worship in Taizé.

At the same time, in no way does the prayer attempt to create a vague and superficial emotional "high" in the participants. It is indeed rather low key, and the content is also very important. Almost everything that is spoken or sung is taken from the Scriptures. Singing verses from the psalms over and over again allows them to be interiorized, and the Bible readings are chosen for their centrality and accessibility. Outside of the worship, during the daily Bible reflections given by the brothers, more difficult texts can be explained and reflected upon. And in Taizé, Bible study is not separated from prayer: the brothers wish not simply to communicate intellectual knowledge, but rather to facilitate the discovery of a personal relationship with Christ.

One of the terms often used by the young pilgrims to describe the experience of worship in Taizé is the word "freedom." "The prayer here is so *free*," they often say. This can seem strange at first hearing, since the liturgy of the community is at the opposite extreme from what is usually called "free prayer." Each service is crafted in advance; the order of worship does not change, and there is little improvisation. Upon reflection, it seems clear that what they mean by "free" is the creation of a space that leaves room for body and soul to breathe. First of all the body: there are no pews in Taizé; most of the participants sit on the floor in a variety of postures. After the service properly speaking, especially in the evening, the singing continues, and one can come and go as one wishes. One can sing or simply listen to the others chanting, in an atmosphere particularly conducive to inner discovery. The time of silence offers a more explicit space of freedom, which one can fill as one chooses, provided, of course, that one does not disturb others. It seems almost paradoxical that the set organization of the prayer favors the creation of an open space where body, mind, and heart are liberated; one discovers that a structured existence and freedom need not be mutually opposed but that, undertaken correctly, the former can make the latter possible. In our contemporary society, where an absence of limits and direction creates an illusion of liberty that is ultimately disappointing, this is a valuable lesson.

SIMPLICITY

A final key aspect of the gatherings in Taizé is the simplicity noted by so many of the participants. In this case, as in many others, this arose first for practical reasons: life in Taizé is simple because that is the only way that the community can welcome so many people. With no sources of funding beyond the modest contributions of the participants and the work of the brothers, the material side of life must be kept basic. The young sleep in cabins with bunk beds or in tents; the food is wholesome without being fancy. There are few distractions outside of the worship, the group meetings, and personal conversations. And yet this simplicity of life seems to offer a refreshing alternative to young people who come from societies drowning in excess, where nothing ever stops, where there is no time just to be, and to be together. They discover that it is possible to be happy without an overabundance of consumer goods; they enjoy being together without being burdened by expectations to meet or busy schedules to follow. Although a lot happens in the course of a day in Taizé, there is no sense of rushing from one thing to the next; there are no deadlines to meet. The Italians have a good word to express this kind of simplicity; they call it *essenzialità*, which can be loosely translated as "focusing on what really matters."

In Taizé there is no gap between the public and the private spheres, and this, too, offers a significant contrast with life in the surrounding society. There is indeed time for solitude and personal reflection, and time for working and sharing with others. But it is obvious that these dimensions both point to an underlying unity. Many young people, like their elders, are searching for such a unity, not a uniformity imposed from without, or one that is achieved by shearing off whole dimensions of existence, but the integrity that springs from a common source able to unify the myriad aspects of life without doing violence to them. To put it another way, many are looking for a faith that is one with their life, rather than a "religion" occupying a clearly delimited domain. As a young man from Senegal who spent two months in Taizé put it, "My experience at Taizé shows me that religion and life are not two separate and independent spheres set side by side. At Taizé, you can be 100 percent young, listen to the music other young people do, dress like they do, and yet make your life a fully Christian life."

This focusing on what is essential certainly favors human relationships, fostering a relaxed atmosphere of acceptance and friendliness that prepares the ground for the growth of true friendship. Coming from cities characterized by anonymity and the fear of strangers, many visitors are astonished the first day to see that everyone says hello and people speak to one another while waiting in line for meals! In such a climate of trust, it is not hard to open up to others and to make friends. "I was surprised," said Rodica, a young woman from Romania who visited Taizé, "to see that a discussion in Taizé can be at the same time quite ordinary and quite profound. It is not rare during a discussion, despite language problems, to speak about personal questions almost without realizing it, sometimes even intimate subjects."

What happens in the small discussion groups is another example of how limits can paradoxically benefit sharing: because the participants speak different languages and must sometimes struggle to express themselves, there is less danger of encountering others on a purely verbal or ideological level, whether to debate or to agree. One is forced to find simple words to express the core of one's convictions and questions, shorn of verbose rationalizations, and this means that the sharing often goes to the heart of who we are and who we want to be.

SEEKERS OF COMMUNION WITH ALL

Toward the end of every week in Taizé, participants in the meetings are gathered together by country or region to reflect on the relationship between what they have experienced and their life back home. What have they discovered, and how can they put it into practice in a very different situation, where they live and work side by side with many others who do not see things in the same way?

Finding ways of making the link between a short and intense experience of prayer and community life, on the one hand, and "ordinary life," on the other, is a common concern in pastoral work today, notably with the young. What can be done to ensure that the flame does not go out in those immersed in a society with quite different priorities, or belonging to a local church that cannot offer the same possibilities for keeping one's faith alive? Moreover, we live in a world that emphasizes the ephemeral, one that favors a great variety of short-term experiences while having little interest in continuity and commitment. The question then becomes even more pressing: is an experience like the one in Taizé doomed to remain short lived, at best to awaken nostalgia for a different kind of life without making it possible to lead that life over time?

People have sought solutions to this dilemma in different directions. In general, they attempt to create structures that ensure continuity over time: series of regular events to participate in, specific proposals to be put into practice in one's everyday existence, commitments by which one promises to follow the indications given and thus to consider oneself as part of a larger whole. This search for structures of continuity is, to a great extent, inevitable, since it corresponds to the incarnate nature of human beings. One cannot simply remain in a perpetual state of spiritual enthusiasm; moments of intensity do not last as such. High points must be translated into the rhythms of daily life, so that, little by little, they can penetrate the depths of the personality and transform it over time. We need the regularities provided by external supports, by the presence of others walking alongside us, to keep our inner searching alive. Brother Roger, for his part, was well aware of this dynamic:

> *Enthusiasm, fervor, is a positive force, but it is by no means enough. It burns itself out and vanishes if it does not transmit its momentum to another force, deeper and less perceptible, which enables us to keep on going our whole life long. It is indispensable to ensure continuity, for times of enthusiasm alternate with periods of lifelessness, arid deserts.* (DP 68-69)

Indeed, it was precisely the wish to make possible continuity over time that led Brother Roger to envisage the creation of a community of brothers linked by a lifetime commitment. And when young people began coming to the hill of Taizé in large numbers, he saw the need to support them in their searching even once they had left Taizé. It was this that gave rise, first, to the "Council of Youth," in the early 1970s, and later on to a "pilgrimage of trust on earth" involving meetings and visits on different continents. It was essential for the young not to feel abandoned in their searching:

> *The questions [of the young people] were hard, and they keep on recurring: "What should we do once we return home to our different countries?" And I found myself unable to give them any real answer. I soon decided that we could not go on without some kind of reply. If we just keep on telling them "go back and carry on from where you are," that becomes an excuse for not trying. In spite of ourselves, our lack of any answer and our refusal to undertake some action means that we are pushing many of them into agnosticism. So it became essential to find a means of staying together, provisionally, yet over a certain period of time, and of asking one another the same questions all over the world . . . (F 17)*

The very same need has led to the birth and existence in the church of many different spiritual organizations and movements, which have often fostered revivals of faith in times when it was in danger of weakening. But Brother Roger took a different tack. He continued,

> *. . . without in any sense creating a new movement. Taizé has never founded any movement, just as there will never be a "Taizé theology" or a "Taizé spirituality." Taizé is simply the name of a monastic family. (F 17)*

This clear limit set to the endeavor to create structures of continuity, difficult for many to understand, flowed from the particular history and vocation of the community. In their attempt to live as a sign of reconciliation at the heart of divided Christendom, the brothers were careful from the outset not to be seen as a "new church" or another denomination. Instead of bringing Christians together, the attempt to create parallel structures would have simply added to already existing divisions. Indeed, as the first brothers knew at first hand from the history of their own churches, Protestantism has suffered greatly from this dynamic of separation: as soon as differences or conflicts arose, each group tended to go its own separate way. The brothers thus wanted to do everything possible to make a clean break with this process of separation and help Christians enter upon a process of reconciliation.

So, while looking for ways to help the young visitors continue their faith journeys upon their return home, the brothers have always refused to create an organized movement around Taizé. Already in 1975, during a "Day of the People of God" held during the summer months, Brother Roger emphasized the local church as the locus of continuity. There could be no question of setting up "Taizé groups" in parallel to existing groups or movements. Not a few eyebrows were raised at the sight of a monastic community sending people back to their parishes and congregations. But the community saw this as essential for it to be consistent with its vocation to be witnesses to reconciliation among Christians.

What Taizé offers the young visitors, then, is essentially an experience of friendship—friendship with God, in a prayer rooted in the heart, and friendship with others across ethnic and religious boundaries of all sorts. They are certainly invited to continue and deepen this twofold friendship upon their return home, and the brothers of the community wish to support them in this. But the community feels it to be essential for this common undertaking to remain fluid and open. Taizé remains a place to which the young can return to deepen their searching, and meetings similar to the ones in Taizé are held regularly in cities around the world, in conjunction with local churches. In addition, since visits among believers have been a way of reinforcing bonds of communion since the time of the Acts of the Apostles, the brothers seek to return the visits they receive, going to join young people in their local churches for times of prayer and reflection. But there is no attempt to recruit members to join an organization or to distinguish those who "belong" from those who do not. As Brother Roger often insisted, Taizé is only the name of a village in Burgundy where a small community of brothers lives, works, and prays.

The refusal to create any parallel structures, while it may impede to some extent any calculation of immediate "results," in the long run favors the search for a wider communion. Those energized by a stay in Taizé are invited to go out and make contact with others, and to do so without any ulterior motives. They are impelled to look for ways of sharing what they have received with their local Christian communities. In addition, it is up to them to invite others from different backgrounds to join the search for communion with God and fellowship with other believers. And so, in many cities, young people have thus started monthly meditative prayers open to all, where people from different Christian traditions and other searchers can come together in the presence of God.[46] In this way Taizé hopes to foster a network of sharing and friendship that can help bring together divided Christians and to set a humble sign of peace and mutual understanding at the heart of the human family.

5

"I Call You Friends"

In this final chapter, taking my cue from the logic of a number of Saint Paul's letters (though evidently without pretending to any special authority), I would like to draw some practical conclusions from the foregoing reflections, passing so to speak from the indicative to the imperative mood. To put it in a nutshell: what does our examination of what Christianity is suggest about the way we are called to live as Christians? How can we "conduct [our] life together (*politeuesthe*) in a way worthy of the Gospel of Christ" (Philippians 1:27)?

Let us first recapitulate briefly the argument of these pages. They began with the question "What is distinctive about the Christian faith?" That question led to an examination of various possible answers, organized according to an increasing degree of relevance.

Although it offers a response to the religious questions of humankind, faith in Jesus is other and more than a religion, if by this are meant beliefs and practices limited to a particular domain of existence, confined to a time and place symbolized in our civilization by "church on Sunday morning." It is likewise more than just a personal spirituality, though it does provide guidelines for living one's life twenty-four hours a day. Perhaps it would be closer to the mark to say that the Christian faith is a way of living together with others, as long as we do not limit this to people whom we know personally and with whom we feel comfortable. The "life with others" to which Jesus invites us is both deeper and more inclusive than anything we can reasonably imagine, since, in the final analysis, it is rooted in God's own identity and being.

We finally reached the conclusion that the Christian faith is essentially the *offer in progress of a universal communion or fellowship in God*. The God revealed by Jesus is a communion of persons, a sharing of life, and this God invites creation to full participation in that same shared life. On the one hand, this communion is *universal*, since in the image of God, it knows no limits. But, on the other hand, it is not abstract but concrete, since it involves the personal choices made by particular men and women to enter into a relationship with God and with their fellows. On this earth, these two aspects of the faith, its universality and its concrete and personal dimension, have to coexist in a fruitful tension with one another, and that means that Christianity inevitably has a *historical* dimension. In other words, the way that this communion is lived out at any given moment is, of necessity, not a fully adequate expression of its true identity; the fellowship of believers is on the road toward a fullness that it will never reach in this world here below. The Christian faith is thus by its very nature an *offer in progress*, a constant process of deepening and expansion, not without momentary setbacks.

If the heart of the Christian message involves living in fellowship with God and among human beings, then it stands to reason that the fact that Christians are gathered into a community is of primary importance for their faith. The church is far more than just the milieu in which people can discover the Good News that comes from Jesus, make it their own, deepen their understanding of it and celebrate it; it is already a privileged expression of that Good News. Christians do not just *go to* church or *belong to* a church; they are only Christians to the extent that they *are* the church, the gathering together by God of those who set out to walk in the steps of his Son. When Saint Paul calls the church the Body of Christ, he is referring to the ongoing presence of the Risen Lord in history inviting people to be reconciled with God and their fellows. The church is both the means of continuing God's work in the world and the necessarily incomplete expression of that work. As the Second Vatican Council expressed it in concise fashion, the church is "the sacrament, or in other words the sign and instrument, both of a very closely knit union with God and of the unity of the whole human race" (Constitution on the Church, *Lumen gentium*, 1).[47]

What does it mean, then, to "be church" in this sense? Although the New Testament and the Christian tradition offer many different images and concepts to illuminate this question, the conviction expressed in these pages is that for our time, the notion of friendship is particularly helpful in pointing a way forward. The basic thesis of this book can thus be formulated in this way: the clearest expression of the Christian faith, as the *offer in progress of a universal communion or fellowship in God*, is a worldwide network of friends, who are at the same time friends of God by being friends of Christ. Drawing their inspiration from the message and life of Jesus, Christians are called to *make friends* with all people and to *be friends* with all who accept their invitation. In the following pages, let us try to grasp what this way of understanding the church could mean in more practical terms.

A Church without Structures?

We must begin by dealing with one basic objection that cannot fail to arise when the church is defined as a network of friends. By speaking in this way, are we not limiting ourselves to one particular type of church organization? Are we not pleading for a Christian community that is as unstructured as possible, with no hierarchy or even formal ministers? It is significant in this regard that the one Christian body that explicitly calls itself the Society of Friends, more popularly known as the Quakers, has gone as far as possible in this direction, eschewing formal leaders and liturgical worship and placing the accent on the "inner light" shining in the heart of each man and woman. Is this type of church organization the inevitable consequence of our reflections? Were this the case, this vision would be incompatible with the theology of ministry and sacraments, as well as the conception of authority, held by the major proponents of the Christian tradition in both East and West. Moreover, when we consider that the Quakers have always remained small in number, we can legitimately ask ourselves whether the image of a group of friends is even applicable to the larger worldwide Christian denominations. In short, is it theologically justifiable, and even realistic, to view the Christian faith primarily from the standpoint of relations of friendship?

The objection just stated is salutary, in that it provides the opportunity for a welcome clarification of our thesis. Rightly understood, the vision of the church as a network of friends neither justifies nor invalidates a particular church structure; it lies on a completely different level. In itself such a vision is compatible with many diverse types of church organization, which must therefore be evaluated on their own merits and on the basis of other criteria.

The clearest way of understanding the different levels involved is to borrow some categories from the medieval theology of the sacraments. This analogy is particularly apt in the light of the words from Vatican II quoted above, describing the church as a sacrament. Early attempts to understand what a sacrament is, beginning with Saint Augustine, saw it as an outward sign made up of tangible symbols, words, and gestures—in short, a particular rite, pointing to an invisible divine reality. Augustine thus distinguished between the *sacramentum*, the sign per se, and the *virtus sacramenti*, its spiritual fruits. Other theologians called this second dimension the *res sacramenti*, the reality of a spiritual order that the sacrament both signifies and realizes.

It gradually became evident that such a twofold distinction was not adequate to elucidate the actual workings of a sacrament. By the time of the great scholastic syntheses of the twelfth and thirteenth centuries, culminating in that of Saint Thomas Aquinas, it seemed necessary to distinguish not two but three different levels: in addition to the *sacramentum tantum*, the rite taken in itself, and the *res tantum*, the ultimate reality, there was added a third dimension, called a bit awkwardly the *res et sacramentum*. This referred to an intermediate reality signified and realized by the liturgical celebration (hence *res*), which, in its turn, signified and realized an invisible divine reality (hence *sacramentum*). So in the Eucharist, *sacramentum* referred to the bread and wine consecrated by the celebrant—in short, to the celebration of the Mass; *res et sacramentum* to the Body and Blood of Christ discerned by faith and received by the communicant; and *res* to Christ's ultimate reason for instituting the Eucharist, namely, to enable believers to root themselves more deeply in the communion of his body. In the same way, for baptism, *sacramentum* was the rite involving water, *res et sacramentum* the change in the recipient's identity, henceforth part of Christ's Body as a member of the church (the so-called baptismal character), and *res* the effects of this new identity as the person's life was transformed by this communion with God ("sanctifying grace"). In typical scholastic fashion, these three levels are distinguished, so as better to understand how a sacrament functions, but never separated; they remain aspects of one and the same event. And we should also point out that the distinction is emphatically not one between human and divine activity, since the sacrament in all of its aspects is instituted by Christ.

If we now, in analogous fashion, apply these three levels to the life of the church, viewed as a sacrament of God's presence and activity in the world, we are easily able to reply to the above objection:

sacramentum	people united and organized by means of structures and ministries, performing rites, undertaking activities
res et sacramentum	community growing in friendship with God through Christ and living in the world as an inclusive society of friends
res	humanity transformed by the Spirit and united to Christ as his Body, thus participating in the communion of the Holy Trinity

This diagram demonstrates that whereas the question of church structure and ministries is situated on the first level, our topic describes second-level behavior and is thus theoretically compatible with a number of first-level possibilities. Or to put it more exactly, the purpose of the first level, in other words, the sacramental and ministerial life of the church, is precisely to foster the growth of a community of friends that, in its turn, manifests on earth (always imperfectly, "on the road," as it were) the *koinōnia* of the invisible God. To emphasize friendship in the life of Christians is thus in no way to downplay the role of church order, but rather to situate it correctly. It has always been understood, in fact, that what is here called the first level of church life is not an end in itself but, however important it may be in day-to-day existence, exists only for the sake of the other two levels. This truth finds clear expression in the constant conviction across the centuries that "when the consummation comes, the sacraments will be employed no more."[48]

It remains true that, here on earth, as incarnate beings we are in need of material signs and social structures to organize our existence, even in the spiritual realm. Already in the Gospels we see that Jesus did not simply call his disciples one by one but formed them into a community with a rudimentary structure right from the outset (the Twelve; Peter, James, and John; Peter). The other New Testament writings, in turn, reveal how quickly the communities of the faithful began to live a patterned life. At the same time, although the vision of the church as a network of friendship does not invalidate the need for sacraments and ministry, it does provide an important criterion for judging their fruitfulness. Do they foster an increase of friendship first of all with Christ, and concomitantly with our fellows? Is authority exercised in a way not to draw attention to itself but as an irreplaceable means for "building up the Body of Christ" (Ephesians 4:12; see also 2 Corinthians 10:8; 12:19; 1 Corinthians 14:3-5,12)? To what extent do ministers of the Gospel fall under Jesus' reproach to the religious authorities of his own time, when he explains their unbelief by the fact that "they receive glory from one another and do not seek the glory that comes from the One who alone is God" (John 5:44)? Or do they take instead John the Baptist as their model to emulate, the one who wished for Christ to become greater and himself to become less (see John 3:30)?

There will always be a need for different ministries in the church; Saint Paul's image of the body clearly indicates that unity in Christ does not suppress diversity. The apostle even goes so far as to shock our modern egalitarian sensibilities by affirming that one can and should accord different respect and honor to different members, though his scale of values is distinct from and even antithetical to that of the surrounding society (see 1 Corinthians 12:22-26). Among the various ministries, pride of place should certainly be given to that which calls believers, in the name of Christ, to sit around his table and share in his Body and Blood so as to realize their identity more and more fully. This being said, our reflection in these pages may perhaps offer some indications regarding the way in which ministry is to be exercised in the church. If the touchstone is friendship in Christ, then any view of the ministry as a caste apart, conferring a superior status, is to be excluded. Friendship does not necessarily imply equality in all areas; it can, and indeed, should coexist with respect and acknowledgment of the particular gifts of each man and woman.

But if we remember that the *koinōnia*, the common element that makes us friends in Christ, is far more basic than the varied roles we play in building up the community, then all forms of clericalism will be nipped in the bud. Once again, Saint Augustine put it most succinctly when he said, "*Vobis sum episcopus, vobiscum sum christianus.* For you I am a bishop; with you I am a Christian" (Sermon 340).

FRIENDS OF GOD

Although friendship is a universal human reality, there is a particular type of friendship that defines what it means to be a Christian: we are friends of one another because we are friends of Christ and thus, implicitly, friends of God.

The notion of friendship with Christ or God is not always an easy one to grasp. First of all, there is the fundamental distinction between the Creator and the creatures, which seems to preclude such a word being used to describe the relationship between the two.[49] But the notion of friendship with God is no less shocking than another teaching that lies at the very heart of the Christian faith—the Incarnation. Christians hold as one of their basic tenets the literally unimaginable claim that in the man Jesus of Nazareth, God himself entered into the ongoing history of the world he created. It is this divine descent or "self-emptying" (cf. Philippians 2:7), motivated solely by love, that makes it possible to speak of a certain equality and reciprocity, which can be fittingly described as friendship and which plays itself out against the background of an even greater difference. As thinkers of the first Christian centuries never tired of repeating, in Christ God became what we are, so that we might become what God is.

To understand the Christian notion of friendship with God, we must thus take as our starting point the fact that it results from the free and unmerited decision by which God leaps over all the barriers and makes a reciprocal relationship possible. The first barrier is the one already mentioned, that between the Source of all being and those who are "called from nothingness into being" (cf. Romans 4:17), in other words who exist by receiving their being from another; this humanly unbridgeable gap is overcome by the mystery of Bethlehem. But there is another barrier even more commonly emphasized in the Christian writings than that between Creator and creature, namely, the refusal of human beings to acknowledge their true condition of dependence, leading them to claim a false autonomy and resulting in an estrangement from the ground of their being. The establishment of a relationship with God therefore requires not just the overcoming of a difference of nature but, in addition, the healing of a situation of alienation or estrangement, traditionally referred to as sin. In the steps of Saint Paul, Christian theology refers to this healing using terms such as *salvation* (see Romans 1:16; Ephesians 1:13; Philippians 1:28; 1 Thessalonians 5:9), *redemption* (see Romans 3:24, 8:23; 1 Corinthians 1:30; Ephesians 1:7; Colossians 1:14), *reconciliation* (see Romans 5:11; 2 Corinthians 5:18-20), and *justification*, the establishment of a right relationship with God (see Romans 3:24-26, 5:1; Galatians 2:16-17; Titus 3:7). These expressions all refer to that fact that, in the life, death, and resurrection of Jesus culminating in the gift of the Holy Spirit, which renews the human condition from within, God changes human beings from enemies into friends.

It is God, then, who takes the initiative in making human beings his friends. But it is clear that any friendship worthy of the name cannot exist unless it is mutual. In contemplating Jesus Christ, we see someone who benefits fully from a relationship of love with the one he called Abba—he is "the beloved Son" (Mark 1:11, 9:7) who receives everything from the Father (see John 3:35, 5:19-20, 8:28-29)—but also someone who responds appropriately. In his steps, Christian life or spirituality can be described as *the attempt to appropriate and deepen a friendship with God through Christ.* How is this done? The short answer is: through word and sacrament. In baptism we say yes to God's offer of friendship, in reading and meditating upon the Scriptures we deepen the meaning of this friendship, and in the Eucharist we discover that being in communion with God by partaking in Christ's Body and Blood reinforces our friendship with all who are on the same road. To these classical means should be added what was referred to earlier as "the sacrament of the brother": friendship with God is deepened and expressed in the love we shower on one another, particularly the neediest.

Friendship is characterized by attentiveness to the other person, and in our relationship with God; this is what we call *personal prayer.* There are perhaps as many ways of praying as there are believers, but they all involve turning our hearts and minds to the Source of our being. Jesus encouraged his disciples to entrust everything to God with the confident trust of a beloved child in his or her parents (see Luke 11:9-13). Without the internalization of a relationship with God through regular moments of prayer, we fail to develop, or quickly lose, the awareness of the presence of a friend who accompanies us through thick and thin. In today's hectic society, people find it much more difficult to take the time to stop and turn to God than in an earlier, less complicated age. The same thing, incidentally, is true for our relationship with other people, and that is undoubtedly one of the reasons that deep friendships and united families are rarer today than ever before. This should lead us to question our priorities; we may discover that a great deal of our "busy time" is actually filled with meaningless bustle. But it may also help to realize that, for prayer as well as in relationships with others, it is not so much the *amount* of time spent as its *quality* and *regularity* that is found to be important in the long run. One of the lessons of the monastic life is that creating and remaining faithful to a rhythm of life is an incomparable help in becoming the persons God meant us to be. When prayer becomes part of the warp and woof of existence, it ultimately comes to define who we are. In this respect, a few minutes a day of intimacy with God, regularly maintained, accomplishes more than short-lived bursts of fervor that inevitably become nothing more than good intentions.

It should be emphasized that speaking of friendship with God or Christ does not mean necessarily *imagining* them in the guise of a human friend. While in some forms of prayer imagination can play an important role—the "composition of place" in the Spiritual Exercises of Saint Ignatius of Loyola comes most readily to mind—people differ greatly in their ability to employ their imagination. And Christian thinkers have constantly affirmed that the realities of God are beyond all human imagining (cf. 1 Corinthians 2:9). Does this make any experience of God impossible? In this respect the age-old notion of the "spiritual senses" can come to our aid: although the unaided physical senses cannot perceive

God or Christ, faith transforms our sensibility to enable a perception of spiritual realities on a completely different level.[50] Without lowering the Son of God to the status of a "buddy," we can, through prayer, grow in the conviction of a supportive and loving presence that never abandons us, to which we can constantly entrust our deepest sorrows and joys, and which helps us to find our way through the labyrinth of a world alienated from its deepest roots.

Some believers have taken this perception of an invisible companion very far, as is shown in this prayer by Peter the Venerable, abbot of Cluny in the twelfth century:

Jesus will always be with me, and he will never turn away from me at any time. Certainly not at any time, for, despising and rejecting all that is not he, I will attach myself to him alone. Jesus will be my life, my food, my rest, my joy. He will be for me my country and my glory. Jesus will be everything for me: here below as far as possible, in hope and love until the gate of eternity: then I shall see him face to face. He has promised.[51]

In the Eastern Orthodox tradition, this divine presence, mediated through Christ and, in his footsteps, by all the holy women and men who have gone before us, notably Mary the *Theotokos* ("God-bearer"), is manifested by the icons that fill the churches and play such a key role in Eastern Christian spirituality. In the ancient churches of the West as well, this use of sacred images is visible in the mosaics that cover walls and ceiling. In the cathedrals of Monreale and Cefalù in Sicily, for example, an immense mosaic of Christ in the act of blessing fills the space above the apse, reminding one of the conclusion of the Gospels of Matthew (28:16-20) and Luke (24:50-51). Does not this architectural feature express a profound truth of the faith, indeed the deepest meaning of Jesus' ascension? As we go further in a personal relationship with the Risen Christ, we discover that he is not far away, as a more superficial understanding would have it. With the eyes of faith we begin to discern him everywhere, until the entire cosmos gradually takes on the features of a friendly presence, and the universe, having become a face, smiles.

AND SO FRIENDS OF ONE ANOTHER

"I call you friends. You are my friends if you do what I command you. What I command you is this: that you love one another" (John 15:15, 14, 17). According to John's Gospel, friendship with Jesus becomes mutual when it leads to relationships of friendship with the men and women whom God has placed on our road, notably with those who have heard and responded to the same call.[52]

Here we need to return to a distinction already sketched out in this book. Developing a relationship with Christ and being transformed by his love leads us to see the whole world as lovable, to strive for relationships of love that exclude no one. In the language used here, friendship with God through Christ is manifested by an attitude of *friendliness* toward all, and this attitude takes tangible form in the endeavor to *make friends* with all those with whom we come into contact, even those who humanly speaking have little in common with us or are hostile ("our enemies").

But if we are invited to *make* friends with all, we can only *be* friends with those who accept the offer and respond in kind. In the course of our life, then, relationships of friendship will thus vary according to the degree of mutuality that is possible, on a continuum going from a somewhat superficial goodwill to deep intimacy. In the writings of Saint John, we have seen that one type of human friendship takes on particular importance, namely, that between all the friends of Jesus. This emphasis on loving "one another" of the Johannine Jesus expresses a fundamental truth: the clearest sign of Christ's ongoing presence in human history is a community of believers, the quality of whose life together shows that divine love can, in fact, transform the world and turn it into God's family. In short, the capacity of the church to communicate the Gospel stands or falls with its identity as an inclusive community of friends.

The consequences of this simple truth are far reaching. In a society where doing, organizing, and achieving reign, how many congregations are aware that, along with deepening a relationship with Christ, building friendship among the members should be a priority? In today's world, such an effort could easily seem a waste of time, taking resources and energy from other, more measurable tasks. And yet the loneliness and individualism secreted by a society where relationships tend more and more to be determined by economic activities—wage earning, consuming, buying, and selling—create in many people a longing for simple bonds of acceptance with no ulterior motives, one that is often not satisfied by their families of origin. In general, it is the smaller, more recent Christian denominations that seem to have responded best to this need. Their character of an extended family always there for their members, especially in times of need, is often what attracts new converts to them, as well as people fleeing from more traditional and anonymous church settings. In these newer communities, if members are not seen at church for a week or two, another member will check up on them; if someone is ill or out of work, a group will visit in order to provide whatever material and spiritual sustenance is necessary. Without always realizing it, these churches are recreating on the basis of faith in Christ the culture of belonging, which was once a staple of our small towns and neighborhoods and which has gradually been eroded by increasing mobility and the breakdown of traditional values in a globalizing world.

The historical or mainstream churches have more trouble satisfying this need to build friendship among their members. First of all, it is their size that militates against this. A large urban or suburban parish, where people see each other only for an hour a week on Sunday morning, is not an ideal place to form deep ties. For this reason, a first step is perhaps to subdivide the congregation, not primarily to accomplish specific tasks (such groups have always existed in a parish, and always will) but as building blocks on the way to creating community.

The diocese of Nanterre, on the outskirts of Paris, has understood this, and has chosen as one of its four major orientations that of "promoting small fraternal faith communities." The animators explain,

Christians cannot live without community. (...) But in the parishes of our diocese, the faithful are quite numerous! It is impossible to know everybody. How can each baptized person receive from other Christians true support for their faith and offer their

own? (...) Today perhaps more than ever, it is necessary that, between the "baptized individual" and the "parish community," there is an intermediate reality of community in which a limited number of people can help each other to live the Gospel in a more direct and regular way and propose it to those who are looking for meaning. (...) This reality is not new. Many different kinds of such communities exist. (...) The present situation calls us to support and develop the ones that work, and to begin, to "invent," new ones.[53]

They further explain that such communities should tend to become places of prayer and sharing around Scripture, although sometimes they may start out just as simple support groups for their members. As "cells of the church," they should not see themselves as independent, but rather they should be linked to a larger community such as the local parish or diocese, so as not to become "a cocoon or a sect." They can take many different forms, from offshoots of existing groups and movements to spontaneous initiatives. The important thing is for such small faith communities to be places where "the joys and the troubles of life are shared, in the light of the Word of God."[54]

This initiative of a French Catholic diocese calls to mind the "house church" movement in Protestantism. In both cases there is the attempt to create smaller groups that offer both spiritual and human support to their members. These communities give the practice of the faith a human face and encourage it by making believers accountable to one another, something particularly important in societies that have drifted far from the teachings of the Gospel. One thinks immediately of the situation of the early

Christians, who met in people's homes and whose life offered a clear alternative to the values of the surrounding empire. If the church is to rediscover its identity as a community of friends, could not such local initiatives, however modest, be an important step in that direction?

COMMUNITIES OF HOSPITALITY

Although in our day it is urgent and advantageous to foster the existence of small Christian communities of all sorts, of house churches and congregations that put an emphasis on relationships of friendship among their members, this is nonetheless not without its own drawback. The text from Nanterre quoted above rightly cautions the communities not to become "a cocoon or a sect." Over time, it can happen that groups where "people feel good together" begin to withdraw inward and make the "feeling good" an end in itself. The clearest symptom of this regression is a reticence to change one's ways, an unwillingness to be open to anyone from the outside who comes and brings something new. Slowly but surely, then, friendship in Christ becomes limited to merely human affability, not to say simple gregariousness; by losing its rootedness in Christ, it becomes both more superficial and less inclusive. One of the criticisms sometimes heard about certain congregations, particularly in affluent areas, is that, from the outside, they look more like social clubs than signs of Christ's presence in the world. Without delivering a verdict on the soundness of these accusations, it is true that emphasizing fellowship among the members to the detriment of everything else can lead to a weakening of the church's overall message. Christian communities, after all, are not called to be coteries of the like-minded, but rather signs of a transformed humanity.

What can be done to guard against this deformation? Three different and complementary paths help to deepen and broaden fellowship among Christians.

The first lies in a "return to the sources," in recalling what is specific about such fellowship. We have repeatedly seen, from Aristotle on, that all friendship is based on a *koinōnia*, a "third factor" held in common by the friends. In the case at hand, this third factor is not a particular human interest or object but the Risen Christ, made present in the community by the activity of the Holy Spirit. "Where two or three are gathered together in my Name, I am there in their midst," said Jesus (Matthew 18:20). To put it succinctly, Christian friendship is friendship *in Christ*. It must thus endeavor by all means possible to keep the living Christ as its focus. This means rooting itself in prayer, in reflection on the word of God, in the celebration of the sacraments, particularly the Eucharist—all realities that point beyond the human dimension of the community to what gives it its identity and cohesion. "You did not choose me; I chose you," Jesus told his followers (John 15:16). Keeping Christ at the center does not mean continually thinking or speaking about him, something unnecessary and even impossible, but simply living in the awareness that if we are together, it is because of Christ's call to manifest him by the love we share among ourselves and with all those with whom we come into contact.

This brings us to a second means of living as friends in Christ. In the Gospels, two groups are considered special friends of Jesus. In addition to calling his disciples friends (John 15:15), he is also known as "a friend of tax-collectors and sinners" (Matthew 11:19).[55] Indeed, one of the most powerful images of community in the Gospel is Jesus sitting at table with these individuals excluded from polite society, while the religious folk and the theologians look on in dismay (see Mark 2:15-17). Similarly, in the great tableau of the "final judgment" (Matthew 25:31-46), Jesus identifies himself with two groups: those who are needy and rejected by their fellows and those who disregard their own comfort to go toward them.

All this seems to suggest that, in the wake of Jesus, a privileged place in the fellowship of believers should be given to "the poor" in the widest meaning of the term—the materially disadvantaged, to be sure, but also all those who are outsiders and unable to find their place in the wider society, whether because of a personal limitation or because of the prejudices of the majority. If a Christian community is open to the poor in this extended sense, it will have found a potent antidote to the danger of becoming too comfortable or of turning inward as a kind of mutual admiration society.

Now it is hard to deny that, down through the ages, the Christian church has been unrivalled in its concern for the deprived. Followers of Jesus have inevitably been found at the forefront of initiatives aiming to feed the hungry, shelter the homeless, take care of the sick, and so forth. And in our time, we have come to realize more and more that, in addition to caring for the victims of social ills, it is essential to work for changes in society that will make these ills less widespread and oppressive, by taking a stand against so-called structures of injustice. Our reflections here indicate, however, another step forward that needs to be taken if we are to be faithful to our founder's vision. Jesus' example shows us that it is not enough to help the poor and outcast; we are asked to make friends with them. Offering assistance from a position of implied superiority merely reinforces social distinctions and confirms the apparent inferiority of those who receive help. This ultimately patronizing attitude, however well meant, is probably one of the reasons why the beautiful word "charity," which originally referred to the selfless love characteristic of God, has become almost an insult in our day.

What would it mean for Christian congregations and communities not just to see excluded individuals and groups as potential clients, objects of care or assistance, but where possible to invite them in as welcome guests, as potential friends? Or at the very least, not to approach them from a position of superiority, but to realize that the relationship is one where we have as much to receive and to learn as to give? When Jesus, tired and thirsty from his travels, met a woman beside a well in Samaria, he did not begin by emphasizing his own superiority as a Jew, a male, and one sent from God, but rather he asked her for some water to quench his thirst, thus occupying the lower place as the object of her "charity" (see John 4:6-7). Such a change of outlook would do much to transform the friendship between believers into an authentic image of God's all-inclusive family.

It must be admitted that this way of acting has never been easy to put into practice. We see this already in one of the earliest writings of the New Testament:

My brothers and sisters, do not have the faith of our glorious Lord Jesus Christ while practicing favoritism. For if an individual en-

ters your assembly with gold rings on his fingers and luxurious clothing, and another one enters who is poor and whose clothes are filthy, and if you look at the one wearing fancy clothes and say, "Sit here and make yourself comfortable," while to the poor man you say, "You can stand over there or sit down on the floor," are you not practicing discrimination among yourselves and becoming like judges with corrupt minds? Listen, my dear brothers and sisters, did not God choose the poor of the world to be rich in faith and heirs of the Kingdom which he promised to those who love him? But you show no respect to the poor. (James 2:1-6)

Expressed in more general terms, one of the imperatives that keep Christian communities on the straight path of the Gospel is that of practicing *hospitality*. It has often been remarked that the Greek and New Testament word for hospitality is *philoxenia*, literally "friendship-love of strangers," whereas today hospitality usually means offering a welcome to friends and relatives. Many, if not most, ancient civilizations considered the need to offer food and shelter to the passing stranger a sacred duty. This injunction found an expression in myths concerning gods coming down to earth disguised in human form and asking to be welcomed, a motif that left its mark on the Bible too, in the story of the three divine messengers who come to Abraham and announce to him the birth of a son (see Genesis 18:1-16).[56] We find an echo of this in the Letter to the Hebrews: "Do not neglect hospitality, for through it some have welcomed angels unawares" (Hebrews 13:2).

The early Christians were called to practiced hospitality especially to fellow believers, in the many visits they made to each other to strengthen bonds between communities in different places.

The practice was so widespread that it gave rise to abuses; we find warnings in the early Christian writings concerning visitors who come for long stays simply to benefit from the free room and board! This tradition of hospitality was kept alive, above all, in monastic communities: first for fellow monks and secondarily for anyone coming to share the monks' life for a time. As the numbers of visitors increased, communities were eventually forced to organize this welcome in a way that did not disturb the daily rhythm of the monastic life. Visitors were then welcomed in *xenodocheia* or *hospitia*, hospices under the administration of certain monks. Here we find the beginnings of an institutionalization of Christian hospitality, which led in a direct line to the charitable institutions so characteristic of Christianity throughout the ages—homes for orphans and the aged, schools for needy children, hospitals, and so forth.

We can ask ourselves, however, whether this increase in efficiency was not to the detriment of the deeper meaning of hospitality. By delegating the practice of welcoming others to specific individuals and groups, the Christian community as a whole lost one more opportunity to keep in mind an important dimension of its existence: the fact that it did not exist merely for itself and its members. In welcoming the stranger we welcome Christ, and this not only gives us the opportunity to practice generosity but also calls us out of our comfortable routines and asks us to open ourselves to something new and often unsettling. Hospitality is a strong reminder that communion in Christ can never be a simple society of the like-minded. As should already be abundantly clear from these pages, the Gospel radically undermines the eternal human tendency to split into an in-group and an out-

group (see Luke 6:27-36). Although it is obvious that, in practice, the offer of hospitality cannot be unlimited if a community
is to maintain its existence and its identity, one of the key signs
that it is living in the dynamic of the Gospel lies in its readiness
to let itself be "disturbed" by those from the outside who may at
first seem alien and even threatening. "I was a stranger and you
welcomed me" (Matthew 25:35).

Servants of Unity and Universality

A third way of keeping Christian groups and communities from
turning inwards in an attitude of complacent self-satisfaction is
for them to strengthen their connections with the rest of Christ's
Body. As mentioned earlier in our discussion of catholicity (see p.
54f), a church in one location is a microcosm of the whole, and
thus a local expression of the Body of Christ, only if it remains
in communion with other local churches. Again, the image of the
cells of a body can be helpful here: though each cell potentially
has all it needs to regenerate the whole organism, in actual fact it
is only fully alive when linked to all the other cells that make up
the body. Smaller groups especially, such as base communities and
house churches, need to maintain a living relationship with the
wider church, such as the local parish or diocese, if they are not to
wither or become sectarian.[57]

Historically, to indicate this wider belonging has been a primary function of the apostolic or pastoral ministry in the church.
In addition to keeping all the different groups or factions within
a local community oriented in the same direction, the bishop
(*episcopos*: "overseer, supervisor") serves as an important link

with the church in other times and places. The importance of this function was recognized very early; it goes back at least to the generation immediately following the New Testament writings. In the early second century, Ignatius, bishop of Antioch, on his way to martyrdom in Rome, wrote a series of letters to the leaders of the churches in the towns he was passing through. His fundamental concern was church unity, and he saw this as guaranteed locally by the link with the figure of the bishop, surrounded by the presbyters (council of elders) and assisted by the deacons:

> *All of you should follow the bishop, as Christ the Father, and the council of elders, as the apostles; show respect to the deacons as the commandment of God. No one should do anything regarding the Church without the bishop. The only Eucharist considered valid should be one celebrated by the bishop or someone he designates. Wherever the bishop appears, there the community should be, just as wherever Christ Jesus is, there is the catholic Church.* (Letter to the Smyrnians, VIII, 1-2; cf. Ephesians IV-VI; Magnesians VII; Trallians II; Philadelphians II, IV)

This unity manifests itself preeminently in the celebration of one Eucharist, where the community in all its diversity is united around the same table.

The bishops, in turn, express the unity between local churches spread across the world, so that Ignatius could also write,

> *I have taken the initiative to encourage you to go forward in harmony with the mind of God, for Jesus Christ, our unfailing life,*

is the mind of the Father, just as the bishops, established to the ends of the earth, are in the mind of Jesus Christ. (Ephesians III, 2)

This role of the apostolic ministry became even more explicit in the following centuries. In the middle of the third century, Cyprian, bishop of Carthage in North Africa, wrote,

And this unity we ought firmly to hold and assert, especially those of us that are bishops who preside in the Church, that we may also prove the episcopate itself to be one and undivided. (...) The episcopate is one, each part of which is held by each one for the whole. The Church also is one, which is spread abroad far and wide into a multitude by an increase of fruitfulness. (On the Unity of the Church, 5)

Among themselves the bishops form a "college," a kind of "parable of communion," which periodically becomes visible in church synods, councils, and today in national and regional bishops' conferences. At this point, we can understand the significance of a question asked by the founder of Taizé at a time when the community was accepting its first Catholic members, regarding the particular ministry of the Bishop of Rome:

If it is true that every local community needs a pastor to renew the communion between people ever inclined to scatter, how can there be hope of a visible communion between all the Christians of the whole world without a universal pastor? (SC 70)

In writing these words, Brother Roger did not fail to recognize how difficult it would be for Christians to agree on an answer to this question:

> *Of course the Bishop of Rome is weighed down with an enormous burden of history, which at present still makes it hard to glimpse the specific features of his vocation. Today he is called to rid himself of local pressures in order to be as universal as possible, in order to be free to express prophetic intuitions. And free as well to exercise an ecumenical ministry which fosters communion between all the Churches, even calling upon those who refuse his ministry. Perhaps the "servant of the servants of God" has a responsibility not just for Catholics, but for non-Catholics too.* (SC 70-71)

Some twenty years later a Bishop of Rome, John Paul II, surprisingly and perhaps unknowingly echoed Brother Roger's concerns in an encyclical letter he wrote on ecumenism:

> *As I acknowledged on the important occasion of a visit to the World Council of Churches in Geneva on 12 June 1984, the Catholic Church's conviction that in the ministry of the Bishop of Rome she has preserved, in fidelity to the Apostolic Tradition and the faith of the Fathers, the visible sign and guarantor of unity, constitutes a difficulty for most other Christians, whose memory is marked by certain painful recollections. To the extent that we are responsible for these, I join my Predecessor Paul VI in asking forgiveness. (...) For a great variety of reasons, and against the will of all concerned, what should have been a service sometimes manifested itself in a very different light. But...it is out*

of a desire to obey the will of Christ truly that I recognize that as Bishop of Rome I am called to exercise that ministry.... I insistently pray the Holy Spirit to shine his light upon us, enlightening all the Pastors and theologians of our Churches, that we may seek—together, of course—the forms in which this ministry may accomplish a service of love recognized by all concerned. This is an immense task, which we cannot refuse and which I cannot carry out by myself. Could not the real but imperfect communion existing between us persuade Church leaders and their theologians to engage with me in a patient and fraternal dialogue on this subject, a dialogue in which, leaving useless controversies behind, we could listen to one another, keeping before us only the will of Christ for his Church and allowing ourselves to be deeply moved by his plea "that they may all be one... so that the world may believe that you have sent me" (John 17:21)? (Encyclical letter *Ut unum sint*, 88, 95-96, May 25, 1995)*

These lines show a clear awareness that the apostolic ministry in the church—whether presbyteral, episcopal, or papal—is not primarily a matter of juridical structures and human institutions organizing one part of God's people. It is rather, at least potentially, a gift given by Christ to build up the faith, hope, and love of all believers, notably by helping them look beyond their local belonging and encouraging them to place their specific gifts at the service of a wider unity. What new ways can be found here and now to make this gift shine forth in its full Gospel splendor, so that it can bear as much fruit as possible, without waiting for the hypothetical day when all Christians are integrated into the same church structures? To go back to our earlier distinction (see p. 120ff), ministry in the church is a first-level reality (*sacramentum*); its reason for being is revealed insofar as it fosters the growth of a worldwide network of friends in Christ (*res et sacramentum*) that, in its turn, expresses a universal communion in God (*res*).

FRIENDSHIP BEYOND BORDERS

In the contemporary world, there is another factor that helps believers go beyond geographical borders and discover the possibility of a more universal friendship. It is not rooted in the Gospel as such, but rather in the evolution of human society. I am referring to the transportation and communication revolution that is part of what is today called globalization. Relatively inexpensive and accessible long-distance travel, and especially the World Wide Web, have made the notion of "the planetary village" more apt than ever before. For example, pilgrims come to Taizé from all across the world, and after their stay, they are effortlessly able to remain in contact with friends made on the hill via e-mail and other Internet-based forms of communication. Ironically, today it is often easier to maintain one's ties with people on the other side of the globe than with one's next-door neighbors.

These recent developments offer impressive tools to discover communion in Jesus Christ as a "world wide web" of friends. They can thus contribute to a deeper understanding of the church as it has in fact implicitly been from the very beginning, in obedience to Christ's call to "go and make disciples from all nations" (Matthew 28:19). The words of Saint John Chrysostom, writing in the fourth century, have taken on a whole new resonance in our day: "He who lives in Rome may look on the Indians as his own members."[58] In a world where instant communication between Europe and Asia is taken for granted, this is no longer merely an abstract possibility.

That being said, it is important not to let the glitter of new technology blind us to technology's very real limits and possible abuses. These can be summed up in the adjective "virtual," which has acquired a new lease on life thanks to the Internet. Closeness and community via electronic communication are "virtual" insofar as they create an impression of sharing and togetherness that is less real than it seems. We cannot, in the end, deny the incarnate nature of human beings: true communion is ultimately rooted in a sharing of life that takes bodily presence seriously and that normally involves physical proximity over a length of time. The experience of many couples who first met one another on the web is an eloquent testimony to this. There is an important and indispensable transition to be made between sharing e-mails and speaking via the Internet, or even flying to a faraway city once a month, and attempting to live together day after day. Virtual intimacy can often undergo a rude awakening when confronted with the wear and tear of everyday life.

In short, while modern means of communication can extend and keep alive a feeling of connectedness with other believers across the world, that connectedness cannot do without unmediated face-to-face encounters. Jesus tells us that we cannot say we love the invisible God if we do not love our brothers and sisters whom we see (see 1 John 4:20). Analogously, how can we say that we love our brother or sister via the Internet, if we are not able to love those we encounter every day? Although it is true that Saint Paul and the other early Christian leaders maintained deep ties with communities across the Mediterranean world via letter, they visited these communities as often as they could and shared their life for significant periods of time (e.g., Acts 18:11, 20:31). The historian and philosopher Ivan Illich, commenting on the parable of the Good Samaritan, eloquently explains how the newness of the Christian message involves seeing the man or woman in need who crosses my path as a brother or sister in Christ. Their physical presence calls me out of my complacency and makes me willing to welcome and assist them; when this assistance is mediated through institutions to increase its efficaciousness, it is thereby on the road to being debased, becoming an anonymous "law."[59]

This is not to say that institutions are not necessary in human life, or that technological advances do not offer suggestive new possibilities for broadening our outlook. After all, our ancestors used tools to extend their reach from the beginning of their existence on this planet. But it is good to remember that the tools we use are not neutral. They take on a life of their own, and almost inevitably end up changing us and modifying our original intentions.[60] It is no longer unusual to see a couple walking down the street with each one conversing with a third party on a cell phone or teenagers sitting at a table in a café not in conversation with one another, but all staring at and constantly playing with small electronic screens that they carry in their pocket or bag. And many people have noted that communication via e-mail or such inventions as Facebook and Twitter, and their eventual successors, diminishes in quality in inverse proportion to its ease. These electronic means, while testifying to a real desire especially on the part of the young to be part of a network of friendship, and offering new possibilities for this if used judiciously, run a great risk of reducing "friendship" to a form of gregariousness, or even conformism, which is extremely superficial and in the final analysis disappointing.

In the face of such a transmutation of human beings into disembodied bits of information, it is salutary to recall the sacramental nature of the Christian community. We enter it by being immersed in water and anointed with oil in the presence of others; we maintain it by receiving Christ's Body and Blood under the appearances of bread and wine. And we should not forget that the word was originally read aloud and explained in the midst of an assembly gathered for worship; the transition to the written word following the invention of the printing press and mass literacy, while offering new possibilities for study and understanding, detracted from a sacramental vision of God's word binding the hearers together into a community of faith. The Judeo-Christian tradition reminds us that we ignore our bodies with their five senses at our own peril. In short, while we should welcome new possibilities of transportation and communication as a way for us to discover the church as a worldwide fellowship in Christ far beyond our local parish or congregation, we need to be attentive to their real limits. A virtual faith-community, to be authentic, must be an extension of flesh-and-blood relationships. If I am not open to the face of Christ in those I see day by day, with all of their defects, can I really say that people across the world whom I only touch electronically or occasionally are truly my friends?

PHILIA AND EROS

After having explored the breadth of friendship in Christ, the time has now come to say a word about its depth. It should be recalled that the classical Ciceronian understanding of friendship tended to limit it to a few close relationships. The friend was an alter ego, another self: how could such a relationship, requiring an enormous personal investment, be extended beyond a small circle? The Gospel arrived on the scene and subverted this perspective, proclaiming the humanly paradoxical possibility of universal friendship in Christ. Does this imply that particular friendships are no longer of importance to believers in Christ, that they are secondary or even proscribed, as has sometimes been the case in some Christian environments?

The most convincing argument against such a devaluation of personal friendships among Christians comes from the Gospel itself. Countless commentators across the ages have brought out the fact that Jesus himself did not relate to everyone indiscriminately. Without calling into question his unlimited love for every human being with whom he came into contact, we see him associating himself with certain men and women in a more intimate way. Among the Twelve, he goes off with Peter, James, and John at particularly important moments (e.g., Matthew 17:1; Mark 5:37, 14:33) and, in the Fourth Gospel, on several occasions we meet the figure of "the beloved disciple" (John 13:23, 19:26, 21:7,20; cf. John 18:15, 20:2), who is identified with the author of the Gospel (John 21:24) and whose identity remains somewhat mysterious.[61] And outside the close circle of his companions, Jesus had a special relationship with Lazarus of Bethany and his two sisters, Mary and Martha (see John 11:5), not to mention the enigmatic figure of Mary Magdalene (Luke 8:2; Mark 16:9), whom we meet especially at the foot of the cross and at the empty tomb. All this seems to make it clear that, in Jesus' eyes, friendship for all does not mean relating in the same way to each person. Every human being is unique, and therefore every relationship between two individuals is likewise unique, as soon as I do not see the other merely as an object who satisfies a certain need in me (Martin Buber's "I-It" relationship), but as a subject worthy of love in him- or herself ("I-Thou"). The Gospel, far from eliminating this basic characteristic of the human condition, takes it into account. In Christ we are indeed called to see everyone as a potential friend, beginning with the one whom I have not chosen but who stands before me and makes a claim upon my attention, but we are not expected to relate to every person in an identical way. Between certain individuals, for reasons that are not always easy to fathom, deeper bonds spring up and grow, a friendship that for believers can take on a particular significance in their history with God.

What we see in Jesus' own behavior in his life on earth has continued throughout the ages in the countless deep friendships between men and women whose lives were dedicated to Christ in a radical way. Far from distracting them from their Christian commitment, these relationships were a privileged expression of it and a support for their existence as followers of Jesus. The earliest example, from the pages of the New Testament, is undoubtedly that of Paul and his co-worker Timothy (see Acts 16:1ff; 1 Corinthians 4:17; Philippians 2:19-23; 1 Thessalonians 3:2; 1-2 Timothy); it is true that Paul uses images from the family ("father, son, brother") to describe the relationship, whereas we would more naturally speak of intimate friends. Paul and Timothy are only the first of innumerable pairs of such friends who have made their mark on the history of Christianity. Basil of Caesarea and Gregory Nazianzus, Perpetua and Felicitas, Francis and Clare of Assisi, Martin Luther and Philip Melanchthon, Fenelon and Jeanne Guyon, John Henry Newman and Ambrose Saint John, Dietrich Bonhoeffer and Eberhard Bethge, Karol Wojtyla and Wanda Poltawska—the list goes on and on.[62]

Of all the different strands of the Christian tradition, it was Celtic Christianity, rooted principally in the British Isles and Brittany, that gave a recognized place to this practice. The Celts even coined a word for it: *anamchara*, which can be translated as soulfriend. The *anamchara*, who could be male or female, lay or cleric, was a kind of spiritual mentor, who took on some of the functions of spiritual direction, counseling, and even confession of sins. Since Celtic Christianity was organized primarily around monastic communities, such friendships were also the preferred method of religious formation: each young monk or nun was assigned to a more experienced brother or sister to foster their spiritual development. But this concept also had a wider application: soulfriendship could refer to any kind of deep relationship between two people that contributed to the growth of faith, wisdom, and the inner life.[63]

It is not rare, in Christian history, to encounter spiritual friendships between a man and a woman who are both dedicated to a life of celibacy for Christ. In today's world, characterized by the omnipresence and the trivialization of sex, questions inevitably arise concerning the character of such relationships; even same-sex ones are not exempt from suspicion. In reading, for example, in a letter of Paulinus of Nola, a contemporary of Saint Augustine, to his lifelong friend Sulpicius Severus,

> *what loss of affectionate devotion can an inhuman parent or an indifferent brother or an inconsiderate friend cause me, as long as everything that goes under these names, either as tokens or bonds of love, is amply repaid to me by you alone? (…) We have had good and great brothers and friends and relations, but the Lord did not wish us to find satisfaction in them; he chose to give you to us as an inseparable brother and a beloved companion, whom we might fittingly love as we do ourselves, since we have one heart and one soul in Christ with you.* (Letter 11, 4)[64]

Are we not quick to suspect homoerotic tendencies and this despite the fact that St. Paulinus was married and later lived a life of asceticism in accord with his wife? And what about these words written by Jordan of Saxony, Saint Dominic's successor as head of the Order of Preachers, to a young woman, Diana d'Andalo:

> *You are so deeply engraven on my heart that the more I realize how truly you love me from the depths of your soul, the more incapable I am of forgetting you and the more constantly you are in my thoughts; for your love of me moves me deeply and makes my love for you burn more strongly.* (Letter 25)[65]

Do we assume that they were obviously lovers? And yet Diana was a cloistered nun who never left her convent, and Jordan, a man who constantly traveled around Europe to visit his brothers in the Dominican order, was together with her in the same place only a few times in his life.[66]

In this area of intimate relationships, the risk of anachronism, of applying modern categories to a world fundamentally different from ours, is particularly great. This is not to say that an erotic component is necessarily absent from all intimate friendships. We can make a theoretical distinction between *eros* and *philia*, romantic love or desire and the love of friendship, to be sure, but, in practice, human beings do not have watertight compartments in their hearts, and so it should not surprise us that there is bound to be some interplay between the two. The problem with understanding our forebears is obviously not that the biological and psychological makeup of human beings ("human nature") has changed, but rather that we live in a sociocultural universe very different from theirs. It is next to impossible for us to grasp to what extent, in previous centuries, people defined themselves and were defined by others through their commitments as part of a clearly structured society. In today's world, by contrast, interpersonal relations are extremely fluid and nonbinding—the notion of a definitive commitment, of fidelity to a given way of life, often seems a vestige of an almost forgotten past. How many people these days are really convinced that marriage is indissoluble? Moreover *eros*, the sublime and all-pervasive longing that in earlier times culminated in the desire for God, has become watered down to mere physical coupling. Like it or not, we are all children of Freud, in the sense that instead of beginning with the summit—in the ancient world *Eros* was the name of a god[67]—and from there heading downwards, we start at the bottom and try to move upwards, if we can. Influenced by the "masters of suspicion,"[68] we tend to regard the higher realms as mere "sublimations" of a basically physical, not to say impersonal and mechanical drive. Whereas our ancestors saw biological sex as a dim shadow or weak echo of a much greater and more significant reality, we consider "libido" as what is real and true, and the rest as essentially scaffolding. This sociocultural context makes it extremely problematic to form spiritual friendships, notably male-female ones, where *philia* is at the center and keeps the upper hand. Such an effort is indeed swimming against the stream, and so it requires significantly greater discernment, self-mastery, and courage than in times past.

At the same time, the rediscovery of the possibility of such friendships could show a way out of the frustration felt by many who, perhaps without realizing it, are longing for a way to reconcile their innate human desires with their quest for fulfillment in God. Those who take the narrow and difficult path of true spiritual friendship realize that, in today's world, they are walking along a knife edge, constantly buffeted by the incredibly powerful winds that attempt to reduce *philia* to the caricature of an *eros* not worthy of its name. This quest is ultimately rewarding, however, not only because it offers a way beyond the sad byways of mere physical dependency, but also for a much more positive reason: by gradually transfiguring our natural longing to love and be loved, deep spiritual friendship becomes another parable of communion in Christ, a microcosm of the church. "Where two or three are together in my Name, I am there in their midst," said Jesus (Matthew 18:20). Vibrant Christian communities where married couples and celibates live side by side in deep friendships could be a powerful countercultural sign, witnessing to the fact—almost unbelievable to many of our contemporaries—that clear limits set to the bodily expression of love do not keep one from finding happiness and fulfillment.

This whole dynamic may become clearer if we start from another side. In the mythology of our day, people consider marriage the archetypical example of a relationship based on *eros*; it is practically taken for granted that if one marries, it is because one has "fallen in love." It is striking to realize, then, that Thomas Aquinas, in the case of the relationship between husband and wife, speaks of *maxima amicitia*, the greatest friendship[69] or alternatively *amicitia intensa*, strong friendship.[70] And, indeed, if physical attraction most often plays a key role in the preliminaries to marriage and in early married life, it should be clear upon reflection that it is not sufficient by itself to sustain a lifelong bond. If friendship does not gradually grow up between the spouses, their faithfulness risks gradually becoming routine or mere duty, and we know how little power duty has to motivate human behavior, especially in our day. Is not one of the most unambiguous manifestations of the beauty of human existence found in certain elderly couples who, after a long life of raising a family, not without struggles and crises, have attained a serene and joyful companionship that eminently deserves the name of friendship? Could not marriage between Christian believers be an ideal setting in which to integrate *eros* with *philia*, and therefore to fulfill Saint Paul's vision of the couple as a sacrament of communion in Christ (see Ephesians 5:31f)? Here it would appear that human *eros* has to call upon *philia* in order to manifest *agapē*.

FRIENDSHIP AND THE ECUMENICAL VOCATION

At the beginning of the twentieth century, after a long period that saw an inexorable decomposition of the Christian community into separate confessions opposed or at best indifferent to one another, a reverse movement began to make itself felt. Fostered by the biblical and spiritual renewal of the previous generations, and by the growing missionary consciousness of many churches, which made their divisions appear all the more counterproductive, believers in Christ began coming together to search for greater unity as a way of being more coherent with their identity and mission. The Catholic Church, at first maintaining an attitude of prudence out of a concern to safeguard the mystery of the faith in its totality, gradually rallied to what came to be called the ecumenical movement; the Second Vatican Council (1962-65) gave it the highest approbation possible. Today, it is part of the ordinary consciousness of the mainstream churches that the current state of division is unacceptable, that a Christian vocation cannot be lived out fully while rejecting or ignoring the multitudes of others who claim to be followers of Jesus Christ.

At the same time, despite this pervasive awareness of the scandal of Christian divisions, it must be said that visible unity seems no closer than before. Indeed, strong centrifugal tendencies have reappeared in all the Christian traditions. The original ecumenical impulse had two dimensions, theological research (Faith and Order) and practical collaboration (Life and Work), and it is easy to see that significant progress has been made in both fields. Serious theological work, often ratified on the highest levels, has been done to clarify doctrinal differences and look for ways beyond them; joint undertakings by Christians of different backgrounds in such fields as working for peace, struggling against deprivation, and assisting minorities in difficulty have become commonplace. And yet the goal of the ecumenical endeavor, "one so that the world may believe," unfortunately still remains elusive.

In recent years, a particular dimension of the ecumenical vocation has received increased attention. It is generally known as "spiritual ecumenism," but this designation would be highly misleading were it taken to imply that the goal was no longer visible communion but a mere inner attitude of tolerance and acceptance of others. The word "spiritual" refers not to the type of unity desired but to the means used to achieve it. By themselves, and however essential they may be, theological reflection and collaboration in practical matters do not reach the essence of what it means to be a follower of Christ. At its most fundamental level, the road to unity in Christ involves a deepening of the spiritual life of believers, both personally and collectively. Here is how the Decree on Ecumenism of the Second Vatican Council put it:

> *[A] change of heart and holiness of life, along with public and private prayer for the unity of Christians, should be regarded as the soul of the whole ecumenical movement, and merits the name "spiritual ecumenism."* [71]

The basic insight here is quite simple: if the divided followers of Jesus wish to work for communion among themselves, they must become themselves persons of communion with God and with their fellows. Intellectual understanding and institutional changes, however important, will never lead to unity as long as the hearts of believers are not transformed by the Gospel call to make God's all-inclusive love a reality in their lives.

For our topic, this means that friendship across denominational lines is a privileged means of bringing about Christian unity. As far as possible, we need to live as if the church were already a worldwide network of friends not limited to those of the same denominational allegiance. Friendship in Christ does not need to wait for full agreement on doctrinal grounds in order to grow. It can even hasten this agreement, because if those reflecting together on the faith are already linked by friendship, their discussions will have less the character of a debate, where each feels called to defend the particular viewpoint of their "team" tooth and nail, and be more a common search for what unites them in depth behind the diversity of accent and approach. Indeed, cannot it be said that every time true doctrinal progress has been made between theologians or church leaders, this has been because the friendships developed among them have made their discussions deeper and more fruitful?

The *Handbook of Spiritual Ecumenism* published by the Vatican's Council for Christian Unity mentions the theme of friendship in several places. In the chapter on parishes and local communities, it states that "wherever Christians live or work together, they can be encouraged to meet in their neighborhoods to deepen everyday relations of friendship, particularly among families."[72] And speaking of pastors, it says that "friendly and fraternal relations between pastoral ministers of different traditions are a primary means of promoting a spirituality of communion."[73] Finally, we hear that monastic communities (and similar things are said of other religious communities and movements) "can offer hospitality and bring together Christians of various traditions in a spiritual family that extends beyond the bounds of the monastery, creating a *milieu* for friendship and ecumenical exchanges."[74]

It is vital to realize that all of these suggestions are not of secondary importance, as if the "real" work of unity were exclusively theological or institutional. As the founder of Taizé for his part understood more and more clearly, reconciliation is a Gospel reality that cannot be put off until tomorrow:

> *The luminous ecumenical vocation is and always will be a matter of achieving reconciliation without delay. For the Gospel, reconciliation does not wait. "When you are bringing your gift to the altar and your sister or brother has something against you, leave everything; first go and be reconciled…" (Matthew 5: 23-24). "First go!" Not, "Put off till later!" Ecumenism fosters illusory hopes when it puts off reconciliation till later. It comes to a standstill, becomes fossilized even, when it accepts the creation of parallel paths on which the vital energies of forgiveness are squandered.*[75]

As soon as the Gospel call to reconciliation is reduced to an activity undertaken by specialized institutions, a task for professionals, it is already betraying its true meaning and purpose.

In a word, beyond the illusions and the disappointments of the ecumenical endeavor, is not an eminently practical and fruitful way open to us, here and now, to respond to Jesus' call to restore unity? Although we cannot immediately resolve the theological disagreements or the institutional barriers to visible unity, we can begin at once to live the reality of the church as a universal network of friends in Christ. In building up spiritual friendships across denominational lines—rooted in intense prayer, a change of outlook by which we go beyond prejudices and snap judgments, and growth in faithfulness to Christ—we already manifest, imperfectly but truly, something of the *res et sacramentum* of Christ's Body. Brother Roger, for his part, was convinced that this renewed spirit of concord could not fail to have an effect on the first level, compelling the structure and institutional forms of the church to mirror more and more its deepest identity as a universal communion rooted in the crucified and risen Lord.

MAKING FRIENDS WITH ALL

This chapter fittingly ends with a topic that is becoming increasingly relevant in our day: the coexistence in the same geographical space of groups with different spiritual practices and beliefs, or with none at all.

Historically, different religions have arisen and prospered in different parts of the globe, to such an extent that they seemed indissolubly wedded to the civilization in which they developed. In most contemporary societies, thanks to the pressures of globalization, people of different backgrounds dwell side by side to an ever greater degree, and so religions other than one's own are no longer perceived as exotic. Moreover, in the West, large numbers of people live their lives with no explicit reference to their Christian or Jewish roots, most often unaware of how deeply these have influenced the sociocultural universe in which they find themselves. In such a pluralistic world, many Christians wonder what their attitude should be.

Two different activities undertaken by believers bring this question to the forefront. On the one hand, Christians very early felt called, in obedience to the "great commission" of Jesus, to "go and make disciples from all nations" (Matthew 28:19). These words express in a nutshell the missionary outlook of the church, and across the centuries they have motivated vast numbers of people to leave their homes in order to spread the Gospel to other societies and cultures. Today, we tend to be more aware, sometimes excessively so, of the limits of this undertaking; we know that, in many cases, along with the message of Jesus, other values and practices were imposed that had less to do with that message than with the exigencies of an expanding European civilization. But although the whys and hows of mission have required rethinking and indeed have already undergone much revision, it is not easy to see how the basic outward-looking thrust of the Christian message can be denied without calling the Gospel itself into question.

On the other hand, increasing globalization has stimulated the desire for mutual understanding and peaceful coexistence. This has led to what is today called interreligious dialogue, whereby Christians, Buddhists, Jews, Muslims, Hindus, and others gather to share on an equal footing. Although such dialogue has many different facets,[76] one of its basic preconditions is that those who practice it come to the table with no ulterior motives. They are not there to prove to others that they are right, that their vision is the only or the best one, but essentially to listen, learn, and share. This does not mean, of course, that they are required to deny or bracket their own beliefs, for in that case, no dialogue would be possible. But such a dialogue requires a willingness to see reality from the viewpoint of others, a readiness to take the imaginative leap of considering on its own terms a worldview radically different from one's own.

The question then inevitably arises of the relationship between these two endeavors. Must Christians forsake the mission of spreading the Good News for the sake of better relationships with others? Alternately, should they renounce dialogue or turn it into a simple pretext for preaching their truth? Or again, are they doomed to live with a kind of split consciousness, undertaking two seemingly contradictory efforts simultaneously without worrying about the way they fit together?

It is to be hoped that those who have followed the argument of this book will understand by now how the vision proposed here offers a way out of this apparent dilemma. The essential message that the church of Jesus Christ wishes to proclaim and communicate, and that it cannot deny without ceasing to be what it is, is that of a universal communion in God. In more concrete terms, this has been translated as the offer of friendship to all. Christians, therefore, fulfill best their calling when they attempt, on account of their faith, to make friends with people from the most diverse backgrounds. And friendship, by its nature, is not self-serving; it is not a means to an end, but rather has its justification in itself.

Whether they are undertaking interreligious dialogue as such, then, or other activities to bear witness to their beliefs more explicitly, Christians are called to show the same basic attitude of disinterestedness. "Freely you have received," Jesus told them, "so give freely" (Matthew 10:8). They are not like supporters of a political party, trying at all costs to attract adherents to their cause, or vendors attempting to convince potential customers that their product is the best. They have received an undeserved and priceless gift, the Good News that in Jesus Christ, God has torn down all the barriers that humankind has erected to full sharing in the divine life, with the consequence that barriers among human beings no longer have ultimate importance (cf. Galatians 3:28). They witness to this Good News first and foremost by attempting to be friends of all, extending a hand even to those who reject their friendship.

This means, then, that in order best to succeed in witnessing to their faith, believers in Christ must constantly examine their own motives. Are they concerned first of all with sharing Good News, by their words but even more so by the way they live, convinced that their message has an inherent power of attraction that can only be impaired in the long run by yoking it to human means of persuasion? Have they uprooted from their hearts all feelings of superiority, remembering that they bear the treasure of the Gospel in jars of clay (cf. 2 Corinthians 4:7)? Do they realize that by listening to others, even those with whom they have apparently nothing in common, they will inevitably learn something to deepen their own faith, something that will help them better to understand the Christ whom they proclaim and whom they claim to live by?

On March 12, 2000, in obedience to the strong conviction of Pope John Paul II, the Catholic Church at its highest echelons celebrated a moving penitential service asking forgiveness for the faults of the church across the centuries. The first one mentioned was announced by then-Cardinal Joseph Ratzinger:

Let us pray that each one of us, looking to the Lord Jesus, meek *and humble of heart, will recogni*ᶎ*e that even men of the Church, in the name of faith and morals, have sometimes used methods not in keeping with the Gospel in the solemn duty of defending the truth.*

And Pope John Paul continued:

Lord, God of all men and women, in certain periods of history Christians have at times given in to intolerance and have not been faithful to the great commandment of love, sullying in this way the face of the Church, your Spouse. Have mercy on your sinful children and accept our resolve to seek and promote truth in the gentleness of charity, in the firm knowledge that truth can prevail only in virtue of truth itself. We ask this through Christ our Lord.[77]

This awareness still has to bear all its fruit in the life of the Christian church. It excludes on principle all means of propagating the Gospel that do not flow from *caritas,* disinterested love, and are not compatible with *amicitia,* friendship. Any forms of physical, economic, or even psychological coercion are at the opposite extreme from the claims of friendship, and thus have no part in the mission of the followers of Jesus. In fact, such tactics harm the very work that they are attempting to accomplish, since they give a false picture of the Christian faith. One can only dream of how different our world would be if Christians had always clung to the conviction that the end, far from justifying the means used, can only be attained by means in full harmony with that end, namely, the creation of bonds of friendship and fellowship in Christ.

We should not imagine, however, that this outlook is only a latter-day discovery. In the late sixteenth century, the Italian Jesuit missionary Matteo Ricci (1552-1610) and his companions practiced an early form of what is today called inculturation. In bringing the Gospel to China, those Jesuits strove to learn the Chinese language and customs, dressed and behaved as Chinese scholars, sharing their knowledge especially in the realm of mathematics and the natural sciences. Ricci attempted to explain Christian dogma to the Chinese not as a new religion but as building on the teachings of Confucius, so important in their country. While we should not discount an element of conscious strategy in this approach to mission, there was, nonetheless, a clear awareness of the distinction between Western civilization and its values, on the one hand, and the truth of the Gospel, on the other, and the corresponding attempt to find points of contact and even convergence with traditional Chinese philosophy. This endeavor did not have lasting consequences, being undoubtedly too far ahead of its time to succeed, but it remains as an eloquent witness to the universal dimension intrinsic to the Christian faith.

"Another very significant aspect of Ricci's life was his insistence on friendship. He was not someone who preached from a distance. He expressed the faith by making friends, by being ready to explain to individual people the hope that motivated him, without imposing his views where they were not welcome. His doors were open to welcome anyone who wanted to visit him. In fact, he received so many visits by day that often his own personal work and prayer—and sometimes even meals—had to be left for the night."[78] Interestingly, this insistence on friendship was one of the only ways that a foreigner could find an entry into a highly structured Confucian society; it was perhaps the one type of relationship between persons that escaped the rigid categories of that world. It was fitting that the first book Matteo Ricci wrote in Chinese and published in China, indeed the first book ever published by a Westerner there, was a *Treatise on Friendship* consisting of one hundred maxims taken from the classical Western tradition. It seems to have been much appreciated by Chinese scholars, and Ricci is still remembered positively in China today.

Closer to us in time, we have already mentioned Charles de Foucauld (1858-1916), the former French soldier and explorer who, in the footsteps of Christ, lived a presence of prayer and humble witness among the nomads of the Sahara desert. His example gave rise, after his death, to several spiritual families in the church who are spread across the globe and attempt to practice the essentials of his way of life. The Little Sisters and Little Brothers of Jesus, and of the Gospel, live in small fraternities in places of poverty and isolation, not to undertake a particular ministry or any form of social work, but to be present as witnesses to Christ through prayer and solidarity among those most forgotten. As Little Sister Magdeleine of Jesus, who founded the Little Sisters of Jesus, wrote to her sisters in 1945,

Like Jesus during his human life, become all things to all people: Arab among Arabs, nomad among nomads, worker among workers ... but above all human among human beings. (...) Like Jesus, become part of the mass of human beings. Penetrate your milieu deeply and sanctify it by sharing its life, by friendship, by love, by a life which is totally given, like Jesus, to the service of all, by a life so mingled with all that you become one with all, wanting to be in their midst like the leaven that vanishes into the dough so that it may rise.[79]

And this way of life, not surprisingly, is essentially one of friendship:

Human friendship, when it is upright and pure, is too beautiful to be destroyed or diminished. You must even—while transforming and purifying it—make it grow in the love of Christ, who embodied the ideal of friendship. And, in his name, you will learn of the great desire for friendship that we must have for all people, going towards them simply because we love them and want to show them this as an end in itself, in other words without expecting any thanks or any results ... even for the apostolate.[80]

In human terms, such a quest for simple friendship with all, particularly those who are excluded from the human community because of poverty, discrimination, or other reasons, may seem useless or utopian. It almost never leads to calculable "results." But if the essence of the Christian message is to witness to a new relationship with the Source of all being made concrete in the existence of one human family, then this endeavor expresses particularly well what it is all about. It shows clearly that Christianity is not one competitor among others looking for adherents in the world marketplace of religions but an expression of "God's folly which is wiser than human wisdom, and God's weakness which is stronger than human strength" (1 Corinthians 1:25).

Conclusion: A Final Parable

There are events that reveal, unexpectedly, the hidden and true meaning of the things we believe and the life we are living. As Brother Roger would have put it, for a few seconds, a corner of the veil is lifted.

On the evening of August 16, 2005, the Church of Reconciliation in Taizé was packed with over three thousand young people in prayer. During the opening songs, a pathological act put an end to the life of the founder of Taizé, who had celebrated his ninetieth birthday three months previously.

At that moment, a first sign appeared. After an instant of confusion and panic, one of the brothers took the microphone and began to sing *Laudate omnes gentes*. Immediately everything quieted down; the liturgy continued as it did every evening, even as Brother Roger's body, close to death, was being carried out of the church. From then on, the hill of Taizé remained at peace. Can we not see this as a subtle indication that the life animated by the Spirit of God is stronger than death, songs of praise more powerful than cries of hatred and fear?

But it was in the days following Brother Roger's death, until his funeral a week later, that the principal sign became manifest. Thanks to modern means of communication, notably the cell phones of those present in the church, the news spread in a few seconds across the entire world. And beginning already the following morning, a host of people began to arrive on the hill, coming from the four corners of Europe and from even further away. Some stayed for a longer time, but most remained only for a few hours, just long enough to remain in silent prayer beside the mortal remains of the founder of Taizé, exposed in the church every afternoon.

To the thousands of pilgrims—some 15,000 were present for the funeral on August 23 in the presence of many church leaders and other dignitaries, with a Eucharistic celebration presided by Cardinal Walter Kasper of the Pontifical Council for the Promotion of Christian Unity—were added countless telephone calls and written messages. All expressed the desire to be associated, even when they could not be physically present, with the celebration of the gift of Brother Roger's life. What was striking in these visits and messages, in addition to their number, was the great diversity of people represented: they came from all the Christian traditions and beyond, from women and men of all nationalities, ages and social conditions, with a large proportion of young people. Thus, in this assembly at the same time real and virtual, a rabbi from Jerusalem went arm in arm, so to speak, with an Orthodox bishop from Romania and a Palestinian family from Bethlehem; schoolchildren from Berlin took their place beside a church leader from Bangladesh and young Serbians; an elderly woman from Cluny, near Taizé, joined her voice to that of the prior of the Grande Chartreuse, of pastors from Geneva, and of a young Muslim from North Africa.[81] Moreover, what all these people expressed was not formal condolences or sentiments displayed for the occasion; evidently touched to the quick by this death, they had an irresistible need to express their communion by a concrete act, even if only a card or a letter. How else can one explain the couple from the South of Italy who, when they heard the news, got in their car and drove for twelve hours to return to Taizé after a twenty-five-year absence, simply to spend the evening in prayer before returning home?

Such an expression of solidarity is, of course, not unique. It is not without precedent for the death of a spiritual leader, especially if it involves violence, to awaken a sense of participation in many: the names of John Paul II, Martin Luther King, and Mohandas Gandhi come most readily to mind. Brother Roger's death was different from theirs perhaps only in the diversity of the people affected and because he was neither a church leader nor someone at the forefront of a liberation movement. In any case, have we reflected deeply enough on the meaning of such "phenomena"? First of all, on a purely human level, they call seriously into question the individualistic mentality so widespread in our day, especially in the West. The fact that we are deeply touched by the death of someone so far away from us demonstrates that the bonds between human beings are just as strong, if not even more real, than the walls we erect to protect our apparent autonomy, to shore up what we call our "self." And let us beware of attempting to explain this as a "primitive" manifestation of mass psychology: the people who expressed their participation in Brother Roger's death were certainly not driven by some kind of collective hysteria. On the contrary, each one's response was eminently personal and intimate. They would not necessarily have imagined that so many others would feel things just as they did; it was only afterwards that they came to realize that they were part of a vast spontaneous movement. These young and not-so-young people experienced an intimate connection, one could almost say a one-to-one relationship, with Brother Roger, even if they had never known him personally.

Seen with the eyes of faith, this death and its aftermath appears as a kind of parable of what the founder of Taizé was searching for his whole life long. It was as if, for an instant, the passing of one man made palpable a worldwide network of friendship and communion, an image of that undivided church for which Brother Roger always strove and for which he gave his life. For a few days, we saw with our eyes and heard with our ears that this fabric of communion, which is the object of our faith, truly exists, that it is not merely a utopia. At the same time, it became clear that it did not arise in obedience to any human calculation: by the gift of his life, Brother Roger acted rather as a "catalyst" that fostered and manifested bonds of communion created in God. The thousands of people who gathered around him were not his own personal friends, but rather friends of God who recognized themselves in him. The grace of his death was that, for a short moment, it made visible what is normally invisible—the action of the Holy Spirit bringing people together here and now. Like the disciples on the Mount of Transfiguration, we were granted, as astonished witnesses, to contemplate with our eyes of flesh a reality of faith. We were enabled to perceive the mystery of the church coming into being, to witness, so to speak, its genesis in God. This allowed us to grasp the fact that the church is one in its very essence, that its unity is a gift that cannot be destroyed by the wounds of division inflicted by human beings.

In addition to being a revelation, this provisional manifestation of a hidden communion, calling to mind the "great multitude" contemplated by the seer of Patmos (see Revelation 7:9), is also a challenge to be met and a task to accomplish. When we compare it to the empirical situation of our churches, burdened by their inconsistencies and sometimes even their scandals, undermined by their divisions and, in some countries at least, on the way to becoming a "tiny remnant" of the elderly, the gap between the two is striking. For this reason there is a strong temptation to set them in opposition, to emphasize one to the exclusion of the other. Some people, accordingly, insist on disqualifying such manifestations of universal friendship around Christ as a surface phenomenon with no true significance, explainable largely on psychological and sociological grounds. At the other extreme, in a society where all obligations or commitments are increasingly viewed as an intolerable constraint, there are many who accord little importance to what they call "the institutional churches," seeing them as an obstacle rather than as a help in living the Gospel of Christ.

This tendency to dissociate life and the structures that organize and support it is disastrous. Were it to succeed, it would discredit Jesus' own mission and give the lie to the Incarnation. It would set up a pernicious disjunction between the action of the Spirit in "God's today" and the continuities by which this action enters into the warp and woof of human history. On the one hand, we would have gusts of wind, short-lived impulses and, on the other, dry bones, mere monuments to the past. That is why it is so urgent to close the circle, to do everything possible to enable the real but often hidden communion with God and among people to correspond more and more closely to the visible gathering of believers, spread out in time and space, that we call the church. Where else can breath find its natural locus if not in a living body?

Here on earth, of course, the church that we see before us and the activity of God's Spirit in human hearts will never totally coincide. Already fifteen hundred years ago, speaking of the visible community of the church, Saint Augustine saw that "many who appear to be outside are within," while "many who seem to be within are without," since, in any case, "the Lord knows his own" (2 Timothy 2:19).[82] Closer to us in time, some people have used this fact to make a distinction between the visible church, where the weeds and the wheat are inextricably mingled, and the invisible church, known to God alone. Those who carried this reasoning to the extreme tended to view oneness in Christ as a spiritual fellowship between true Christians belonging to all the different denominations, and this often led them to downplay the importance of visible unity. In centuries past, however, even the proponents of invisible unity felt a need to take part in the life of a particular faith community. For their successors today, this seems less and less to be the case.

Must we say it once more? Although we can distinguish different levels in a life of communion in Christ, this distinction cannot turn into a separation without misconceiving the human condition and undermining God's work. It is undoubtedly true that ministry and sacraments, together with the whole realm of church organization and structures, are not an end in themselves. They exist ultimately for the sake of building up the Body of Christ, in other words to allow friendship with God and among human beings to develop and grow. This cannot, however, be used as an excuse to neglect these God-given means. Friendship in Christ, although it contains a dynamism that leads it constantly to go beyond our human limits, must be expressed in a visible way, over time, in communities that have recognizable features. In short, no deepening or renewal of communion in God, if it is not to be a mere flash in the pan, can neglect the empirical structures that make this communion tangible.

The Second Vatican Council, in chapter 8 of the Constitution on the Church, *Lumen gentium*, categorically rejected any separation between "the visible assembly and the spiritual community" and affirmed that the church is "one complex reality which coalesces from a divine and a human element." On the Reformed side, we find a similar insistence in these words of Karl Barth:

> *We have no right to explain the multiplicity of the churches as a necessary mark of the visible and empirical as contrasted with the ideal, invisible and essential Church; no right, because this entire distinction is foreign to the New Testament. (…) There is no way of escape from the visible to the invisible Church. Our questioning, therefore, as to the unity of the Church cannot be silenced by pointing away to the invisible or essential Church. (…) In fact, we have no right to explain the multiplicity of the churches at all. We have to deal with it as we deal with sin, our own and others.*[83]

A twofold task thus lies before us: first, to understand the Christian faith more and more deeply as an offer of communion with God and among human beings, made concrete in relationships of friendship between believers and open to all; and, at the same time, to do all in our power for the empirical organization of the church to reflect this basic identity and foster this friendship. In a world that is inexorably heading toward the discovery of its unity, not without vacillations and confusion, what better way can be found for this unity not to be achieved under the sign of political and military hegemony, economic dependency, or ideological uniformity, but in the only manner that is truly human, that of a communion of free persons, of a multitude of friends?

Notes

1 This chapter is a slightly modified version of my article "What Is Distinctive about the Christian Faith?" *Short Writings from Taizé 3* (July 2007), http://www.taize.fr/en_article6778.html.

2 The etymology of the word *religio* remains controversial. Scholars hesitate between *relegere*, "to re-read, to treat or consider carefully" and *religare*, "to bind, link, connect."

3 Quotations drawn from the book by Sabine Dramm, *Dietrich Bonhoeffer. Eine Einführung in sein Denken* (Gütersloh, Germany: Kaiser, Gütersloher Verl.-Haus, 2001), 228.

4 In his earlier years, Bonhoeffer was deeply influenced by the great Reformed theologian Karl Barth, who also undertook a criticism of religion in the name of faith in Jesus Christ. Barth, for his part, considered religion mainly as the attempt of human beings to reach God by their own powers. He affirmed that such a Babel-like undertaking, far from being praiseworthy or even neutral, was, in fact, a formidable obstacle to the salvation that comes from God alone through Christ. By passing through Christ, however, religion can be saved, just like the rest of human existence. This conception of religion, more theological and abstract, differs from that of Bonhoeffer, more historical and empirical.

5 "God, who is rich in mercy, because of the great love of his with which he loved us, made us alive with Christ when we were dead because of our sins—your salvation is a free gift—and raised us up with him and seated us with him in the heavens in Christ Jesus, so that all the ages to come might see how unbelievably great God's generosity is through his goodness to us in Christ Jesus. You have been saved as a free and undeserved gift, through faith. This is not your doing; it is a gift from God" (Ephesians 2:4-8; see also Romans 5:8).

6 Dietrich Bonhoeffer, *Ethik*, quoted in Dramm, 232.

7 Brother Roger of Taizé, *God Is Love Alone* (Chicago: GIA Publications, 2003), 51.

8 In fact, this "triadic logic" is rooted in the human condition. The French philosopher and historian Pierre Legendre has shown convincingly that no society can institutionalize binary classifications except with reference to a "third instance," a source of authority that legitimates them, whether it be called the state, reason, God, or something else. The biblical outlook makes this logic explicit and draws out all its consequences.

9 The Church fathers, and in their footsteps the tradition of the Eastern

Church, speak explicitly of the "sacrament of the brother." For Saint John Chrysostom, the "sacrament of the altar" and the "sacrament of the brother" are as inseparable as love of the invisible God and love of neighbor. In the poor, the ill, the imprisoned, whom we are asked to help, we encounter the real presence of Christ (cf. Matthew 25:40, 45): "Insofar as you did (not do) it to the least of these brothers and sisters of mine, you did (not do) it to me."

[10] Dante Alighieri, *Paradiso*, Canto XXXIII *"l'amor che move il sole e l'altre stelle."* This is the last line of *The Divine Comedy*.

[11] This interpretation is confirmed by Luke's version, which instead of the "good things" of Matthew 7:11 speaks of "the Holy Spirit" (Luke 11:13). Similarly, Luke shows that the "perfection," which Jesus views as characteristic of God (Matthew 5:48), is, in fact, "mercy" or "compassion" (Luke 6:36). See note 12 as well.

[12] This is perhaps the best understanding of the meaning that the Greek word *teleios*, usually translated as "perfect," attempts to express. As shown by the Lucan equivalent in the same phrase, *oiktirmon*, "merciful or compassionate" (Luke 6:36), it is not a question of some kind of moral perfection, a notion not found in the Semitic languages, but of a love that is whole, simple, inclusive. See as well James 2:8f, 13.

[13] If we are to believe the Gospels, sometimes this seemed to have taken even Jesus himself by surprise. During his first foray into pagan territory, he attempted to justify to a Syrophoenician woman the priority accorded to Israel, only to be brought up short by discovering the quality of her trust in him (see Mark 7:24-30).

[14] Sometimes referred to as God's angel or messenger (cf. Acts 8:26, 10:3, 23:8).

[15] For a good summary, see chapter 5, "The Success of Christianity," in John G. Gager, *Kingdom and Community: The Social World of Early Christianity* (Englewood Cliffs, NJ: Prentice Hall, 1975), 114-48.

[16] The term *ekklēsia* gradually supplanted *plēthos*, 'multitude, assembly, whole community' (e.g., Acts 4:32; 6:2). See "The Church: A Biblical Word," in *Letter from Taizé* 2009-3 (Brother Richard). The other possibility, *synagōgē*, never seems to have been a viable alternative, probably because of its already established use within Judaism (but see James 2:2). In the Germanic languages, *ekklēsia* was replaced by *church*, *Kirche*, *kerk*, probably from *kuriakē oikia*, "the Lord's house."

[17] Cf. Henri de Lubac, *The Splendor of the Church* (San Francisco: Ignatius Press, 1986), 103-10. Here we touch upon the topic of the Church as mother, a

theme that runs through the entire Christian tradition. See Henri de Lubac, *The Motherhood of the Church* (San Francisco: Ignatius Press, 1982), 39-168. From an evangelical point of view, see Christopher Cocksworth, *Holding Together: Gospel, Church and Spirit—The Essentials of Christian Identity* (London: Canterbury Press Norwich, 2008), 94-96. This leads Christian thinkers naturally to a consideration of Mary, prototype and model of the faithful believer, as figure of the Church. See, for example, de Lubac, *The Splendor of the Church*, chap. 9, and Cocksworth, *Holding Together*, chap. 5.

[18] For a Greek Orthodox view of catholicity, rich in insights for the Western Church, see John D. Zizioulas (Metropolitan John of Pergamum), "Eucharist and Catholicity," in *Being as Communion: Studies in Personhood and the Church* (Crestwood, NY: St. Vladimir's Seminary Press, 1985), pp. 143-169. Similarly, in the Slavonic version of the Nicene Creed, *katholikēn* was translated as *sobornuju*. The corresponding noun is *sobornost*, which became a key notion in Russian religious philosophy of the nineteenth and twentieth centuries. This rich word, with its overtones of organic community, spiritual sharing, conciliarity and open friendliness, came to express the essential quality of Church life. For a meditation on *sobornost* that is in fundamental harmony with the outlook of these pages, see Bishop Seraphim Sigrist, *A Life Together: Wisdom of Community from the Christian East* (Brewster MA: Paraclete Press, 2011).

[19] C. S. Lewis, *The Four Loves* (Glasgow: Collins, 1960). The Latin equivalents of the last three are *amicitia*, *amor*, and *caritas*. Since the word "charity" in English has degenerated to the point of signifying, for most people today, giving alms to the poor, there is no longer any specific word to designate adequately the love Jesus practices and recommends. In these pages I will use the expressions "Christian love," "*caritas*," and "charity" to express the same reality.

[20] Ibid., 61.

[21] Ibid., 58.

[22] In fact, the strongly triadic nature of friendship is undoubtedly why Lewis considered it less "natural" than other loves. Physical and biological phenomena are dyadic insofar as they can generally be understood according to a schema of cause-effect, stimulus-response, or need-satisfaction. The symbol-making ability of human beings, on the other hand, their capacity for language and perception of meaning, cannot be adequately accounted for by a dyadic model. What makes us truly human is thus the ability to enter into triangular relationships. See Walker Percy, *The Message in the Bottle* (New York: Farrar, Straus & Giroux, 1979).

[23] For the historical evolution of friendship described in this section, I am deeply indebted to the masterful study by Liz Carmichael, *Friendship: Interpreting Christian Love* (London: T & T Clark, 2004). Her book is an indispensable starting-point for any reflection on this topic.

[24] Ibid., 11.

[25] The topic of friendship in Saint Augustine has frequently been studied. In addition to Carmichael, *Friendship*, 55-68, see Edward C. Sellner, "Like a Kindling Fire: Meanings of Friendship in the Life and Writings of Augustine," *Spirituality Today* 43, no. 3 (Fall 1991): 240-57, http://www.spiritualitytoday.org/spir2day/91433sellner.html.

[26] An alternative to the word "monastic," from the Greek *koinos bios*, "common life." This term emphasizes the communal nature of monasticism, whereas the etymology of *monachos*, "single, alone" refers more to its separation from society.

[27] Cf. Augustine's Letter no. 130 to Proba, chap. 6: "Friendship should not be restricted to narrow bounds, for it embraces all to whom love and esteem are due, although we are naturally inclined to love some people more readily and others less so. It nonetheless extends even to our enemies, for whom we are also commanded to pray. It follows that there is no one belonging to the human race to whom affection is not due, if not out of mutual love, still because we share a common nature."

[28] "Whoever has love is born of God; whoever does not is not born of God. This is the great sign, the great principle of discernment. Have whatever you want: if you do not have this one thing, nothing benefits you. Have this and you fulfill the Law. 'Whoever loves their brother or sister fulfills the Law,' says the Apostle. And 'Love is the fulfillment of the Law'" (*Commentary on the First Letter of Saint John*, V, 7).

[29] P. Amédée Hallier, *Un éducateur monastique: Aelred de Rievaulx* (Paris: Gabalda, 1959), 56.

[30] Ibid., 58.

[31] *Spiritual Friendship*, bk I, para. 10, trans. M. Eugenia Laker, Spiritual Commentary by Dennis Billy, C.Ss.R. (Classics with Commentary) (Notre Dame, IN: Ave Maria Press, 2008), 33. References henceforth given as, for example, (*Spiritual Friendship*, I, 10) in the text.

[32] "This friendship, to which here we admit but few, will be outpoured upon all and by all outpoured upon God, and God shall be all in all" (*Spiritual Friendship*, III, 134).

[33] Carmichael, *Friendship*, 105.

[34] Thomas Aquinas, *Summa Theologica*, II-II, 23.1, quoted in Carmichael, *Friendship*, 110. Cf. also: "*Caritas* signifies not only the love of God, but also a certain friendship with him, which implies, besides love, the mutual return of love, together with a certain mutual communion.... This fellowship consists in a certain familiar conversation with God, begun here through grace, perfected in the future life, through glory" (*Summa Theologica*, I-II, 65.5, quoted in Carmichael, *Friendship*, 107).

[35] Op. cit., 72-73, quoted in Carmichael, *Friendship*, 139.

[36] Ibid., 80; Carmichael, *Friendship*, 141.

[37] John Henry Newmann, *Parochial and Plain Sermons* II, 5 (San Francisco: Ignatius Press, 1987), 258. Carmichael, *Friendship*, 150.

[38] Simone Weil, *Waiting for God* (New York: Harper & Row, 1951), 108. Carmichael, *Friendship*, 170.

[39] Pavel Aleksandrovich Florenskii, *The Pillar and Ground of the Truth* (Princeton University Press, 1997), 296. See also Bishop Seraphim Sigrist, *A Life Together*, 69-72.

[40] Jürgen Moltmann, *Kirche in der Kraft des Geistes* (Munich, Germany: Chr. Kaiser Verlag, 1975), 134. Eng. trans.: *The Church in the Power of the Spirit* (New York: Harper & Row, 1977), 115. Translation modified. See Carmichael, *Friendship*, 178-83.

[41] Ibid., 316. Translation modified.

[42] Elisabeth Moltmann-Wendel, *Rediscovering Friendship* (London: SCM, 2000), 86.

[43] Letter to J. Hours, May 3, 1912, quoted in Little Sister Annie of Jesus, *Charles de Foucauld: In the Footsteps of Jesus of Nazareth*, trans. Little Sisters of Jesus (Hyde Park, NY: New City Press, 2004), 75-76.

[44] Roger Schutz, *Introduction à la vie communautaire* (Geneva: Labor et Fides, 1944), 28-29.

[45] References to Brother Roger's writings in this chapter will henceforth be given by the following abbreviations with page numbers: PC, *Parable of Community: Basic Texts of Taizé* (London: Mowbray, 1980, 1984); UP, *Unanimité dans le pluralism* (Taizé, 1966); DP, *The Dynamic of the Provisional* (London: Mowbray, 1981); VP, *Violent for Peace* (London: Mowbray, 1981); F, *Festival without End* (London: Mowbray, 1983); WL, *The Wonder of a Love* (London: Mowbray, 1981); DF, *And Your Deserts Shall Flower* (London: Mowbray, 1983); HT, *A Heart That Trusts* (London: Mowbray, 1986).

[46] In 2007 Brother Alois, the current prior of Taizé, proposed in a "Call for the Reconciliation of Christians" an "ecumenism of prayer": "Let us no longer

waste so much energy in the oppositions among Christians, sometimes even within our denominations! Let us come together more often in the presence of God, in listening to the Word, in silence and praise. Once a month or every three months we can invite those who live in our towns, villages or regions to a 'vigil for reconciliation.'"

[47] Although the language of this affirmation is that of the church in communion with Rome, the content is part of the common patrimony of Christians, namely that the community of believers does not exist for itself but solely for the sake of the communion between God and humankind.

[48] *The Imitation of Christ*, IV, XI, 2, quoted in Henri de Lubac, *The Splendor of the Church* (San Francisco: Ignatius, 1999), 77. Despite the passage of time, Cardinal de Lubac's critical analysis of the "illusion" that views the "visible organism" of the church as something eternal, as an end in itself, still bears careful meditation. See ibid., 73ff.

[49] And yet Islam, which accentuates more than Christianity the unbridgeable gap between God and all else, does not hesitate to apply the expression *Awliya Allah*, "friends of Allah," to certain believers.

[50] For a masterly exposition of this topic, see Hans Urs von Balthasar, *The Glory of the Lord, A Theological Aesthetics: I: Seeing the Form* (San Francisco: Ignatius, 1982), 365ff.

[51] Peter the Venerable, *Sermon to Praise the Lord's Sepulcher*, quoted by Brother Roger of Taizé in *The Dynamic of the Provisional* (London: Mowbray, 1981), 60.

[52] It is true that in John 15:17 Jesus uses the verb *agapō* and not *phileō*. This, however, does not warrant seeing the love we are called to show to other human beings as fundamentally different from the love Jesus receives from the Father and shares with us. We have only to consider the frequency of formulas of the type "Father > Son > believers" in the Fourth Gospel (6:57, 10:14f; 14:10ff, 15:9f, 12, 17:18.21ff, 20:21; cf. Revelation 2:26ff, 3:21) and the regular alternation of the two verbs for love (compare John 3:35 and 5:20, 11:3 and 11:5, 13:23, 19:26, and 20:2, 14:21, 23, and 16:27, 21:15-17).

[53] Gérard Daucourt, *Orientations pour la mission des catholiques du diocèse de Nanterre* (Nanterre, France: Diocèse de Nanterre, 2009), 30-31.

[54] Ibid., 37. It is not the least of the ironies of history that this endeavor of a Roman Catholic diocese bears a striking resemblance to the abortive plan of Martin Bucer, the sixteenth-century reformer of the city of Strasbourg in Alsace. Bucer urged that "pastors ... create and animate small groups of the faithful, in their parishes, willing to be formed in the faith, to exhort one an-

other to love-charity, and to practice among themselves a pastoral discipline of repentance and sanctification. And that, by these *Christlichen Gemeinschaften*, small communities of professing Christians, the Church of the multitude may be little by little reinvigorated, along the lines of the early Church." Gottfried Hammann, *Entre la Secte et la Cité: Le Projet d'Église du Réformateur Martin Bucer (1491-1551)* (Geneva: Labor et Fides, 1984), 79-80. See especially 76-83, 353-86, 410-13.

[55] In Jesus' day, the category "sinners" was as much a social as an ethical one. It referred to all those who, for whatever reason, were unable or unwilling to follow all the prescriptions of the Torah, for example, people engaged in occupations that made them ritually unclean.

[56] On this whole topic, see Claudio Monge, *Dieu Hôte: Recherche historique et théologique sur les rituels de l'hospitalité* (Bucharest: Zeta Books, 2008).

[57] Pope Paul VI, in his Apostolic Exhortation *Evangelii nuntiandi* (December 8, 1975), described well the dangers when communities, on whatever level, become isolated from the wider communion of believers: "As history in fact shows, whenever an individual Church has cut itself off from the universal Church and from its living and visible center—sometimes with the best of intentions, with theological, sociological, political or pastoral arguments, or even in the desire for a certain freedom of movement or action—it has escaped only with great difficulty (if indeed it has escaped) from two equally serious dangers. The first danger is that of a withering isolationism, and then, before long, of a crumbling away, with each of its cells breaking away from it just as it itself has broken away from the central nucleus. The second danger is that of losing its freedom when, being cut off from the center and from the other Churches which gave it strength and energy, it finds itself all alone and a prey to the most varied forces of slavery and exploitation" (§ 64).

[58] St. John Chrysostom, Homily 65, 1, quoted in Henri de Lubac, *Catholicism: Christ and the Common Destiny of Man* (San Francisco: Ignatius Press, 1988), 54.

[59] See *The Rivers North of the Future: The Testament of Ivan Illich as told to David Cayley* (Toronto: Anansi Press, 2005), esp. 47-58.

[60] For his part, Illich distinguishes between three historical periods: a time when tools were literally an extension of a human organ, the discovery of tools as realities in themselves at about the twelfth century in Europe, and the transition to the age of systems at the end of the twentieth century. A computer is not a tool in the classical sense, because, in using it, we are forced to become part of its system. In today's world, we are thus at the mercy of the works of our

hands to a greater extent than ever before. See *The Rivers North of the Future*, chaps. 4, 13, 18.

[61] For a good discussion, see Richard Bauckham, *Jesus and the Eyewitnesses: The Gospels as Eyewitness Testimony* (Grand Rapids: Eerdmans, 2006), 412-71. See also Richard Bauckham, *The Testimony of the Beloved Disciple: Narrative, History and Theology in the Gospel of John* (Grand Rapids: Baker Academic, 2007).

[62] For a recent work exploring a great many such friendships, male-male, female-female, and male-female, throughout the history of Christianity, see Jacqueline Kelen, *Les amitiés célestes* (Paris: Albin Michel, 2010). Intimate friendships also play a key role in the Sufi tradition of Islam, the paradigmatic example being the relationship between the great Persian poet Rumi (1207-1273) and his mysterious companion Shams.

[63] See the writings of Edward C. Sellner, notably *The Celtic Soul Friend: A Trusted Guide for Today* (Notre Dame, IN: Ave Maria Press, 2002).

[64] Paolino di Nola, *Le Lettere, a cura di Giovanni Santaniello* (Naples, 1992), 326-28.

[65] Gerald Vann, O.P., *To Heaven with Diana! A Study of Jordan of Saxony and Diana d'Andalò with a Translation of the Letters of Jordan* (New York: iUniverse, Inc., 2006), 88.

[66] As a matter of fact, both St. Paulinus and Blessed Jordan show us excellent examples of friendship in Christ and never without him. Cf., for example, the following letter of Jordan to Diana: "What is lacking to you because I cannot be with you, make up for in the company of a better friend, your Bridegroom Jesus Christ whom you may have more constantly with you in spirit and in truth…. He is the bond whereby we are bound together; in him my spirit is fast knit with your spirit; in him you are always without ceasing present to me"(Letter 29). Ibid., 93.

[67] And for the Bible, though not a god, desire is what makes us human. It indicates the constitutive openness of our being to the other and consequently finds its highest manifestation in the longing for God (e.g., Psalm 42, 63; Isaiah 64:1). Conversely, God's relationship to Israel is sometimes compared to a marriage (e.g., Hosea 2; Jeremiah 2; Ezekiel 16; Song of Songs). In the New Testament, Jesus' thirst (see Luke 12:49-50; John 19:28) is an expression of his desire to communicate God's love to humanity by giving himself. In the first part of his encyclical *Deus caritas est* (December 25, 2005), Pope Benedict XVI categorically rejects the tendency to separate strictly, and even to oppose, *eros* and *agapē*, a position usually linked to the name of the Swedish bishop and

theologian Anders Nygren. According to the pope, "When the two are totally cut off from one another, the result is a caricature or at least an impoverished form of love" (§ 8). See the illuminating article of D. C. Shindler, "The Redemption of *Eros:* Philosophical Reflections on Benedict XVI's First Encyclical," *Communio. International Catholic Review* 33 (Fall 2006): 375-99.

[68] The philosopher Paul Ricoeur coined this characterization of Nietzsche, Marx, and Freud, whose views of reality articulated and fostered a widespread tendency in our civilization to "explain" the higher by the lower and see less noble motives everywhere at work behind the scenes.

[69] Thomas Aquinas, *Summa contra Gentiles* III, 123, 6; cf. Liz Carmichael, *Friendship: Interpreting Christian Love* (London: T & T Clark, 2004), 108.

[70] Aquinas, *Summa contra Gentiles* III, 124, 5.

[71] *Unitatis Redintegratio*, § 8, quoted in Cardinal Walter Kasper, *A Handbook of Spiritual Ecumenism* (Hyde Park, NY: New City Press, 2007), 10.

[72] Ibid., 74.

[73] Ibid., 87.

[74] Ibid., 82.

[75] Brother Roger, *No Greater Love: Sources of Taizé* (London: Geoffrey Chapman Mowbray, 1991), 21.

[76] For a good introduction, see Brother Johannes of Taizé, *Dialogue and Sharing with Believers of Other Religions: Reflection Based on a Life-Experience in Bangladesh* (Short Writings from Taizé, 4), http://www.taize.fr/en_article7445.html.

[77] http://www.vatican.va/news_services/liturgy/documents/ns_lit_doc_20000312_prayer-day-pardon_en.html.

[78] "A Portrait: Matteo Ricci," *Letter from Taizé* 2010-1 (Brother Jean-Marc).

[79] Petite Sœur Magdeleine de Jésus, *Du Sahara au monde entier* (Paris: Nouvelle Cité, 1981), 410.

[80] Ibid., 414.

[81] For a sample of these testimonies, see *Choose to Love: Brother Roger of Taizé 1915-2005* (Taizé, France: Ateliers et Presses de Taizé, 2007).

[82] St. Augustine, *Multi qui foris videntur, intus sunt; et multi, qui intus videntur, foris sunt. —De baptismo* V, 27, quoted by Henri de Lubac, *The Splendor of the Church* (San Francisco: Ignatius, 1999), 212. Cf. *Enarr. in Psalmos* CVI, 14: *Quam multi non nostri adhuc quasi intus, et quam multi nostri adhuc quasi foris? Novit Dominus qui sunt eius.*

[83] Karl Barth, *The Church and the Churches* (Grand Rapids, MI: Eerdmans, 1936), 36-37, 41, quoted in Hans Urs von Balthasar, *Karl Barth: Darstellung*

und Deutung seiner Theologie (Cologne, Germany, 1962), 16. Cf. also the final document, "Towards a Common Understanding of the Church" (1990), published by the international Reformed-Catholic dialogue: "In the past, Reformed churches have sometimes displayed a tendency not only to distinguish, but also to separate the invisible church, known to God alone, and the visible church, manifest in the world as a community gathered by the Word and Sacrament. In fact, such a distinction is not part of genuine Reformed teaching. We can affirm together the indissoluble link between the invisible and the visible. There exists but one Church of God. (…)The invisible church is the hidden side of the visible, earthly church" (§ 126-27).